The Easy-ish Way
To Lose Weight And Get Fit

by
Ian Rowland

Publication

The Easy-ish Way To Lose Weight And Get Fit

by Ian Rowland

1st edition

Copyright © 2020 Ian Rowland. All rights reserved.
ISBN 978 0 955 8476 9 1

Published by Ian Rowland Limited.

Dedication

I dedicate this book to anyone who has an addiction and also to their loved ones, family and friends.

Let's build a world without addiction.

This Is Free >

This booklet is available free of charge from www.theaddictionfixer.com

It's about what we can all do, every day, to build a world free from all types of addiction, not just weight issues and obesity.

Please download it, copy and share!

Let's End Addiction

Ian Rowland

What we can all do, every day, to build a world without addiction

A Quick Note About Me

I do three things so I have three websites.

www.theaddictionfixer.com

I want to help people to overcome addictions of all kinds. That's what www.theaddictionfixer.com is all about.

- - -

www.coldreadingsuccess.com

This is my website devoted to two types of cold reading. It tells you all about my books on the subject, the training I offer plus a lot of *free* information and downloads.

- - -

www.ianrowland.com

This is about my work as a writer, speaker and trainer. Among other things, it tells you about the talks I offer on 'Unlock Your Mind', 'Practical Persuasion' and 'Overcoming Addiction'. Clients to date include the FBI, Coca-Cola and Google.

About My Addiction Fixer Books

A Range Of Books But Similar Content

I've written a range of books about creating a world without addictions.

This book, 'The Easy-ish Way To Lose Weight And Get Fit' has a fairly self-explanatory title.

I have other books on the website about various types of addiction. The different books contain some of the same information because addiction issues tend to overlap.

I've also written a short booklet called 'The End Of Addiction', which is completely free. It's about the things we can all do, every day, to create a world free from the human carnage of addiction. It's available from www.theaddictionfixer.com in paperback, Kindle and pdf formats.

Please Tell Your Friends

If you want to tell your friends about me and this book, which I hope you will, it helps me if you send them to my own website rather than to the lovely people at Amazon:

www.theaddictionfixer.com

I *have* made this book available on Amazon (paperback only) because these days people think that if a book's not on Amazon it doesn't exist.

However, it's nicer for me if people order from my own website, where you will also find the Kindle version, extra information, free downloads, related products and discount deals not available elsewhere.

So, please direct your friends to me rather than to Amazon if at all possible.

Thank you!

Contents

Part One: The Rowland Reset   **11**

Step 1: Addressing The Basic Question   12

Step 2: How To Change What You Want   14

Step 3: Find Your Food   23

Step 4: Find Your Exercise   37

Step 5: Stay Great   48

The Rowland Reset: Summary   55

How To Overcome Dependency   **57**

About Addiction And Dependency   58

Managing Withdrawal: The PAT Process   60

Part Two: Additional Information

Part Two: Additional Information   **65**

The Ideas This Book Is Based On   66

More About The Want Fix   70

More About Meditation   71

More About Finding Your Food   73

More About Finding Your Exercise   83

More About Staying Great   87

More About Positive Attitudes   90

More About Benefits   102

More About The Information Problem   110

A Typical Contradiction   119

Overcoming Emotional Resistance   120

Find Your Motivation   123

People Management   125

The Four Qualities Of Successful Plans   127

Is This Book Unique?   129

My Story   130

Introduction

Welcome to the Rowland Reset — the easy-ish way to lose weight and get fit.

For most of my life I was addicted to sugar and starch. I fought hard to overcome this addiction but always failed. Tried everything, consulted all the experts, never got anywhere. Unsurprisingly, I ended up obese, reaching 118 kg (260 pounds).

At the age of 56, I found the answer. I discovered how to overcome my addiction, lose weight and get fit the easy-ish way.

I've written this book in the hope that other people don't have to go through what I went through.

Who This Book Is For

If you are overweight and don't want to be, this book is for you.

If you are overweight and happy about it, and don't care about the long-term health implications, then maybe this book is not for you. I'm not trying to *persuade* you to feel unhappy. I'm just here for people who are overweight but don't want to be.

How This Book Works

In Part One, I'll get straight to the point and explain the five steps of the Rowland Reset. I've tried to keep this as short as I can.

In Part Two, I'll give you more information about various aspects of weight loss and fitness. You might find some of these sections useful and interesting. I've kept all this extra information separate in order to keep Part One as brief as possible.

If you're interested in who I am, and how I came up with all the material in this book, you can read 'My Story' at the end of Part Two.

You're Great

Let's get a few things straight.

You're great.

You're not weak, you don't lack willpower and there's nothing wrong with you.

You can lose as much weight as you want and you can do it the easy-ish way. You can get fit too. It's not hard.

You don't have to go on a strange diet, count calories, starve yourself or *ever* feel hungry. You don't have to go to the gym or do any exercise you don't want to do.

You don't have to rely on willpower or hypnosis (and willpower wouldn't work anyway).

You don't need pills, supplements, 'slimming products' or special equipment of any kind. You can just eat normal food from normal shops and stores.

I will keep these promises to you.

Part One: The Rowland Reset

In Part One, I'm going to explain the complete Rowland Reset: the easy-ish way to lose weight and get fit. There are five steps.

Important - Please Read!

I have no medical or therapeutic qualifications.

If you are going to make any significant changes in your life, especially regarding food and exercise, you should first go to see your doctor or physician. Discuss the changes you intend to make and take their advice.

I do not accept responsibility for any aspect of your health. You should not regard anything in this book as medical advice. The contents of this book are only offered as personal testimony, opinion and information. I do not promise or guarantee any specific results or outcome. If you take any of my advice, you do so entirely at your risk and on the basis that every individual is different so results may vary.

Step 1: Addressing The Basic Question

You may think you have a weight problem. You don't.

You have an information problem and it's not your fault.

When it comes to weight loss and fitness, there's a lot of bad information around. This is why some people say it's about going on a diet (wrong), counting calories (even more wrong) or lots of willpower (wrongest one so far). I've heard all this bad information referred to as 'infobesity'.

If you have tried to lose weight and haven't managed it yet, here's the reason: nobody has given you the information you need. I'm going to give you the *right* information.

The thing about losing weight and similar issues is this: if you don't get to the root of the problem, you can't get to the root of the solution. Telling someone to chew on celery sticks or have more willpower or lift some weights isn't going to help.

The root of the problem, in this case, is that you have an addiction. Life can be hard and you have learned to cheer yourself up, and compensate for life's emotional rough spots, using food. How do you overcome this? You start by realising you need a way to change what you feel you want. Let me explain this in a bit more detail.

The Willpower Trap

Imagine a health and fitness expert is advising you about losing weight. Maybe they are suggesting some tips about exercise or what to eat. Consider this for a moment. The things that the expert is recommending are things you either *want* to do or you *don't want* to do.

If they were things you wanted to do, you would already be doing them, right? So, they must be things you don't naturally feel inclined to do.

If they are things you don't naturally want to do, your only option is to try to *make* yourself do them using willpower. This is what 'willpower' means: trying to make yourself do things you don't naturally feel you want to do. (You never mention willpower when it comes to things you *want* to do, like watching your favourite show or tucking into a pizza.)

However, this leads to a big problem. The truth about willpower is that *it always runs out*. It might run out after a few days, weeks or months. It might run out after a year... but it *will* definitely run out. I can even tell you *when* it's most likely to run out. The chances are, it will run out during your next emotional crunch point: a relationship goes wrong, you get frustrated at work, a friend lets you down and so on. If willpower is the tree, emotional crunch points are the chainsaw.

When your willpower runs out, as it certainly will, you will abandon the things you have been trying to make yourself do and go back to your old lifestyle — the lifestyle that led to you being overweight.

Fact: **willpower is no power**. It's not a way to *permanently* lose weight because it's a *temporary* fix and always runs out.

So, let's go back to that imaginary expert advising you about exercises and what to eat. If they were things you wanted to do, you'd be doing them. If you don't want to do them, you could try using willpower but that runs out. It seems like there's no way to win, doesn't it? This is the willpower trap.

What you need is a way to *change* what you feel you *want*.

For example, consider the idea of doing a few exercises. If you don't feel you *want* to do them, you have to rely on willpower which will run out. However, if you could change what you feel you want, so you actually *want* to do the exercises, that would be different, wouldn't it? Willpower wouldn't come into it. This is the key to losing weight.

So, **how can you change what you feel you want?** This is what I refer to as The Basic Question. The answer is to use the technique I'm going to explain in Step 2, called The Want Fix.

It's simple, easy and free, and it works *amazingly* well.

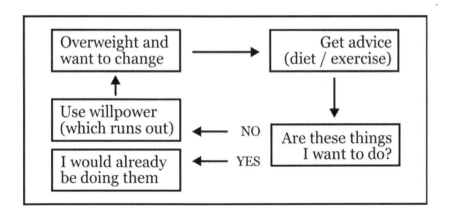

Step 2: How To Change What You Want

How can you change what you feel you *want*, so you never have to rely on willpower? The answer is a technique called the Want Fix.

Get To Know Your Fixer

You know that different parts of your body do different things. Your legs are pretty good for moving around, your hands are good at opening a tub of ice cream and so on. Well, it's the same with your mind. Different parts of your mind do different things. There is one part of your mind that does a very special job: it constantly tries to keep you happy and feeling good. In this book, I'm going to refer to this part of your mind as your Fixer.

Whenever you feel disappointed, frustrated or annoyed, your Fixer tries to make you feel good again. Also, if you're just feeling a bit down, your Fixer tries to make sure you get some pleasure or a sense of reward.

How does your Fixer try to cheer you up? You know the answer. If you like drinking alcohol, it works out the quickest way for you to get some booze. If you like eating sweet things, it figures out the best way for you to enjoy a big sugar feast. Whatever you're into — gambling, smoking or anything else — your Fixer uses it to make you feel better.

By the way, it doesn't matter whether or not you think this part of your mind, your Fixer, really exists. If you prefer, you can just see it as a model, a metaphor or a way of representing an idea. It doesn't make any difference to the Want Fix.

Your Fixer looks after you 24 hours a day, 7 days a week. It's really good at what it does, never stops and never *can* stop. Unfortunately, the work your Fixer does involves two significant problems.

The first problem is that your Fixer only understands short-term results. It doesn't understand or care about long-term consequences. All it cares about is fixing your mood *now*.

The second problem is that your Fixer uses whatever it has learned are the fastest, most reliable ways to make you feel good again. Your Fixer doesn't care whether these are advisable or healthy ways to cheer you up. It just goes with what it has learned usually *works*.

Here's the great news: you can *negotiate* with your Fixer and ask it to do its job in a different way. This is what the Want Fix is all about.

Preparing For The Want Fix

Just before we get to the actual Want Fix process, there's a little bit of preparation for you to do.

First if all, if you don't like the name 'Fixer', you can call this part of your mind anything else you like: your Mood Guru, Emotional Controller, Inner You, Mind Maestro... whatever you want. All that matters is that you have *some* way of referring to it. In this book, I'll carry on referring to your Fixer.

You will also need some way of *visualising* this part of your mind. It's entirely up to you how you do this. You can see your Fixer (or whatever you call it/him/her) as:

- A miniature version of you sitting somewhere in your head or your body.

- A mystical or spiritual entity of some kind, like a 'ghost' version of you that drives your choices.

- An abstract presence, like a source of light or energy.

- A robot, full of wires and circuits deep inside your brain, programmed to keep you happy.

- A well-meaning friend.

- Someone at a large control desk, full of screens and dials, trying to operate your mental machinery.

Choose whatever visualisation works for you. All that matters is that you have some way of visualising your Fixer that you like.

Good. You have a way of referring to your Fixer and visualising it. Now you're ready for the Want Fix.

The Want Fix

The Want Fix involves asking your Fixer to do its job in a different way.

I'm going to explain the Want Fix in five parts. It's best to read through the whole process, so you know how it goes, before you actually try it.

Part 1: Meditate

You need to find about 10 minutes of peace and quiet. Choose any time and place where you can relax and meditate. Just sitting in a comfy armchair or on the edge of your bed is fine.

Relax and focus on your breathing for a while. Enjoy slow, deep breaths, in and out. If you know how to meditate, great. If not, ask a friend, read about meditation online or see Part 2: 'More About Meditation'.

After you have focused on your breathing for a while, say you want to communicate with your Fixer (or whatever name you prefer). This all takes place inside your mind and only involves your inner voice. You *can* speak out loud if you want to but your inner voice is enough.

Your Fixer doesn't have a voice so it can't talk. Invite your Fixer to give you *some* sort of signal that it is listening to you. The response will just be a feeling of some kind: a twitch of your hand or fingers, a sense of part of your mind or body 'lighting up' with attention, a feeling of energy or something else. Just wait until you feel *something* to indicate your Fixer is listening and responding.

Once you have made contact with your Fixer, you can carry on.

Part 2: Give Credit And Gratitude

Give your Fixer *credit* for all the great work it does and express your *gratitude*. In your own words, say something like this:

> "I want to thank you for all the great work you do! I know you work really hard for me, constantly trying to make me happy when I don't feel good. You do a great job and you never let me down. I really appreciate the work you do. Thank you for looking after me so well!"

Wait for your Fixer to give you some sort of feeling or sensation by way of response. Once you have given credit and expressed your gratitude, you can carry on.

16

Part 3: Negotiate

Next, make it clear you are not going to ask your Fixer to stop doing its job. That won't work. It *can't* stop. Ask your Fixer to carry on doing what it does but in a slightly different way. Using your own words, negotiate with it like this:

"I am not going to ask you to stop doing what you do. I love what you do for me and want you to carry on!

However, I'd like you to do your job in a slightly different way. Some of the methods you use at the moment provide fake, short-term happiness, but they have long-term results that actually make me *un*happy. For example, I don't really want to be overweight and unfit. I sometimes feel depressed about it.

I don't want fake, short-term happiness with bad consequences. I want long-term happiness with good consequences. So, please can I ask you to use some other ways of making me feel good?"

Wait for your Fixer to respond in some way. As before, this won't be in words. It will just be a feeling or a sensation of some kind.

Part 4: Suggest Better Ways To Feel Good

Suggest ways in which your Fixer can help you to feel good that will *not* have bad long-term consequences. Obviously, only you know what will work for you. Here are some options and possibilities:

Go for a good walk / visit the beach / go for a drive / visit a place of outstanding natural beauty.

Call a friend you haven't spoken to for a while / meet up with friends and have fun (without doing anything fattening) / chat to a friend on Skype.

Play a musical instrument or learn how to / write a short story / devote some time to a craft or hobby.

Play with your pet / do some 'de-clutter' housework you find satisfying / do some gardening or tend to your houseplants.

Bake or cook something non-fattening.

Watch something funny online / get stuck into a good book / watch TV or listen to a radio show, audio book or podcast.

Feel pampered in some way, such as getting your hair or nails done. Meditate, do some yoga, sip green tea, become enlightened and solve the mysteries of the universe.

Do something silly, fun and frivolous. Alternatively, study for a qualification of some kind and gain a marketable skill.

Join a local special interest group (books, drama, board games, vintage car restoration, ... whatever you're into).

Take part in a faith-based activity at your place of worship if you have one.

Make love with your partner / watch a classic movie / have a nap / take a shower. (I'm listing these as separate choices but, hey, if you can combine all four, great!)

Do some charity or voluntary work so your focus is other people instead of yourself.

Just lie down for a bit or enjoy a short nap.

There are other options that involve exercise, but we'll get to those later.

Just talk to your Fixer and suggest a few ways to make you feel good that do *not* have bad long-term consequences. You are helping your Fixer to do its job in a new, different and better way.

As before, wait for a response from your Fixer.

Part 5: Give More Thanks And End The Session

Thank your Fixer for listening to you and for responding to your suggestions.

Repeat your acknowledgement of all the good work your Fixer does for you. Repeat your thanks and make it clear that you want your Fixer to carry on doing its important and excellent work but in a slightly different way.

Having completed these steps, finish off with some more meditation and breathing exercises. In your own time, allow yourself to come out of the meditative state and back into your normal, conscious awareness of your surroundings.

You have completed your first Want Fix session! Well done!

Maintain The Relationship

Just talking to your Fixer once won't work. It's important for you to maintain an ongoing relationship. In fact, you should have four types of sessions with your Fixer. Let's look at each of the four.

(1) Regular Reminders

On a regular basis, repeat the Want Fix I've just outlined. Meditate, get in touch with your Fixer and go over the same basic points: praise and thanks, negotiation, suggestions and a bit more thanks to finish off.

Having these 'reminder' sessions once a day is ideal, especially when you're just starting your weight loss and fitness journey. If this isn't practical for you, aim for at least two or three sessions a week. They don't have to take long. I generally choose to meditate for about fifteen minutes but you might find that shorter sessions, lasting only five or ten minutes, are all you need.

Each session is a chance to reinforce the new direction you want to take. It's also another opportunity to praise and encourage your Fixer — and we all work better with regular encouragement!

(2) Preparation (For Challenging Situations)

As well as regular reminder sessions with your Fixer, have an extra session whenever there's a challenging situation coming up. A 'challenging situation' is one in which you might feel tempted to go back to your old ways and eat something fattening.

For example, let's say you're planning to meet a friend at a place where, in the past, you tended to eat something sweet or fattening. You can make sure this doesn't happen. All you have to do is use the amazing power of *anticipation* and the 'mental movie' technique.

Here's how to do it. Meditate and get in touch with your Fixer. *Anticipate* what's going to happen and ask your Fixer to handle it in a new, better way. Use your own words to say something like this:

> "Today I'm going to meet [friend] at [place] where, in the past, I usually had some of that [fattening food] that I used to feel would make me happy. Can we please do things a bit differently this time? I want to meet my friend and have a great time, share a laugh or two and come home after... but *without* eating anything fattening. Can we do it this way, please?"

That's the first part. The second part is to play a *mental movie* of the whole situation, from start to finish. See the whole thing in your imagination. You go along, you meet your friend, you have a great time, you make your way home. It's all good — you just don't do the 'eat something fattening' part. You are showing your Fixer a short movie of how you want things to go.

You will be *amazed* at the positive difference this makes. You will still enjoy these occasions (in fact, you might enjoy them *even more* than you did before). You just won't want to eat anything fattening!

(3) Praise Sessions

Whenever your Fixer does well, and keeps you feeling good *without* using the old, fattening methods, take the time to thank your Fixer. This only needs to take a minute or two, although you can spend longer if you want. Communicate with your Fixer in the usual way and then, in your own words, say something like this:

> "I just want to thank you for the way you handled that situation today, and the way that we did [non-fattening activity] instead of [fattening activity]. That was really good! It's exactly what I want you to do! Well done! I'm so grateful to you."

(4) Correction Sessions

Suppose there's an occasion when your Fixer looks after you in the old way. You eat something fattening and you feel a bit of regret afterwards. What should you do?

Have a session with your Fixer. Don't be critical. Be kind, forgiving and encouraging. In your own words, say something like this:

> "I ate [whatever it was] today. This isn't really what I want because it's the sort of thing that makes me overweight. It's all right — you're learning new ways to keep me happy and this is a process of adjustment. It's obviously going to take some time. When I'm in that situation again, please can you handle it this way [suggest a better way of dealing with it]. I'd really appreciate it. You do great work, and I know you're going to get even better at it as time goes by!"

Always talk to your Fixer in your own words and using your own way of expressing yourself. I'm just offering general guidelines. Always keep the tone positive, grateful and encouraging.

Isn't Talking To Yourself Crazy?

Some people say things like this about the Want Fix:

"Isn't it crazy to talk to myself?"

"I would feel stupid just sitting there talking to me."

First of all, there's nothing wrong with self-talk. Millions of people do it every day. There is nothing wrong with it in psychological or psychiatric terms.

Secondly, you're not just 'talking to yourself'. You are using a valid therapeutic technique to connect with a part of your own mind. You're doing it to achieve a positive change in your behaviour and your life. There's nothing wrong with this. In any case, nobody else has to know about it! Negotiating with your Fixer is something you can do on your own when there's nobody else around.

Some people hire me to mentor them through their weight loss and fitness journey. I've never yet had a client who couldn't find some quiet, private time to meditate and communicate with their Fixer. It's not crazy and nobody else needs to know what you're doing.

Fake Happy Or Real?

The Want Fix always works. Literally everyone can benefit from it.

Take a moment to think about this. You have an innate desire to feel happy, content and fulfilled — in fact, to feel as good as you can, as often as you can. This is just part of how we're all wired up.

Your Fixer / Controller / Inner You (whatever you're calling it) knows it can make you feel better with things like sugar, nicotine or alcohol. However, these methods only create *fake* happiness for a *short* time. In the long-term, they have bad consequences. For one thing, they are making you overweight. Also, you're aware that these not-very-good methods will probably lead to horrible health problems.

By using the Want Fix, you are suggesting ways your Fixer can help you feel good *all* the time *without* harmful consequences. (When I say 'all the time', this is a slight exaggeration. Life always has its ups and downs. I'm really saying 'as much of the time as possible'.)

It's a simple choice. When it comes to feeling good, do you want *fake happiness* for a *short* time? Or *genuine* happiness almost *all* the time?

It's Going To Happen Anyway

There's one thing about your Fixer that it's important to understand. You don't get a choice about whether it affects your life or not. It is going to drive your behaviour whether you want it to or not. It never stops and can't stop.

You can believe it's real or not. You can believe it governs a lot of your behaviour or not. Regardless of what you choose to believe, it's going to be there, working 24/7 and doing its best to keep you feeling good.

The only choice you get is this: does your Fixer use the old ways to keep you happy (that lead to bad results, weight gain, health problems and so on) or new, better ways that take you to a happier, better place without any bad consequences. This is your choice. The car is moving along regardless of what you think. All you get to choose is the destination: fake, short-term happiness that doesn't last and leads to problems, or real, long-term happiness that lasts almost all the time.

Progress Check

The previous section was Step 1: 'Addressing The Basic Question'.

This was Step 2: 'How To Change What You Want'. It was about *how* to change what you feel you *want* using the Want Fix. This involves negotiating with your Fixer so that it will use different methods to make you feel good. Basically, it's about realising you don't want *fake* happiness for a *short* time. You want *genuine* happiness *all* the time.

If you want more background information, see Part 2: 'More About The Want Fix'.

What's next? Well, you want to be able to make good suggestions to your Fixer about what you eat. To do this, you need to fix your relationship with food. Don't worry — I am not going to suggest you spend the rest of your life eating limp lettuce leaves and counting calories. Forget all that nonsense.

Step 3: Find Your Food

Let me start this chapter with two promises. I am not going to suggest you go on a diet (because diets don't work). Also, I will *not* try to tell you what you should or should not eat.

If you are overweight and don't want to be, then you currently have a bad relationship with food. It's a bad relationship in the sense that it's producing a result you don't want (being overweight or obese). In this chapter, I'll show you how to fix this relationship so you enjoy your food more than *ever and* lose weight in an easy-ish way.

Three Problems Rolled Into One

Why are you overweight? You might think it's simply and obviously because you eat too much. Here's the newsflash: this is *not* actually why you're overweight. There's *much* more to it. In fact, any so-called 'weight problem' is really three problems rolled into one:

- The information problem.

- The refined carbs problem.

- The awful Western diet problem.

Let's look at each one in turn. Then I'll show you how to fix your relationship with food.

(1) The Information Problem

This is the information age. You have access to books, videos, TV shows, websites, courses and classes galore. Finding out how to eat in a healthy way, and lose a bit of weight, should be easy, right? Maybe it would be if not for Rowland's Law Of Diet Experts: 'For every diet expert, there's another one saying the exact opposite'.

I spent decades of my life trying to figure out what I should eat to lose weight and be healthy. All I found was a chaos of contradictions. Every expert and source of advice seems to contradict all the others. It seems no one can actually agree on what seems like quite a simple question. The more you try to find the answer, the more confusing it gets.

In Part 2, 'More On The Information Problem', I go into this point in a lot more detail. Let's move on to the second problem.

(2) The Refined Carbs Problem

What causes obesity? Some people say it's simply a case of 'calories in versus calories out'. It's fairly easy to see that this isn't true. Suppose that whenever you ate a meal, your body simply took what it needed (for nutritional purposes) and eliminated the rest. If this were the case, you'd never gain any weight, would you?

So, it's not just about how much you eat. It's also about what you *retain*. The fact is, some foods cause your body to store the surplus as fat or, to put it simply, they put your body into Fat Gain mode. Let's look at how this works in very simplified terms.

There's a group of foods called carbohydrates or 'carbs' for short. These are divided into sugars, starches and fibre.

You might think sugar is that white stuff that some people add to tea and coffee. Well, table sugar is *one* form of sugar (called sucrose) but there are several others. Your body's main source of energy is a sugar called glucose, which gets carried round in your bloodstream.

Some carbs are known as 'simple' or 'refined' carbs. Your body can digest these very easily, quickly releasing their glucose energy. Result: they produce a rapid increase or 'spike' in your blood sugar level. You find simple carbs in things like chocolate, fizzy drinks and anything that tastes sweet. They are also found in starchy foods like bread, pastry and pasta — particularly the 'white' versions.

Other carbs are known as 'complex'. Your body has to do more work to break them down and digest them so it takes longer. This means the glucose energy gets released into your blood over a longer period of time, so you don't get the same blood sugar spike. Wholewheat pasta is one good example.

So far, so good:

Simple carbs > your blood sugar level goes up quickly.

Complex carbs > your blood sugar level goes up more slowly.

When your blood sugar levels surge, your body produces a hormone called insulin. Its job is to get your blood sugar level down to what your body considers to be a normal, healthy level. Insulin does this by converting surplus blood sugar into stuff called glycogen that gets stored in your liver. Once your liver is full, which happens fairly quickly, the insulin finds a different solution: it converts the sugar into stuff your body can store in fat cells. This is your body in Fat Gain mode.

24

There's one more part to the story. When you eat a lot of sugar and starch, you trigger the insulin response I've just described. If you do this often, you get a lot of insulin floating around in your blood which leads to *insulin resistance*. Basically, your normal insulin response doesn't have the same effect on blood sugar as before. When this happens, your body tries to compensate by producing more insulin. It's a vicious circle: high insulin causes resistance, which leads to more insulin.

Another hormone called cortisol is also part of the story. I'll come back to this in a later section called 'Fitness And Stress'.

When your blood sugar is low, your body produces different hormones, including one called glucagon, that converts the stuff in your fat cells back into usable energy. This is your body in Fat Loss mode.

So, why are you overweight or obese? It's not *just* that you eat a lot (although you probably do). The main reason is this:

You eat foods that trigger the insulin response so you go into Fat Gain mode (and you have built up insulin resistance).

The main culprits are simple carbs (including various forms of sugar and starch). If you eat these types of foods fairly often, you will gain weight. Unfortunately, avoiding simple carbs in order to lose weight is harder than you might think. For example, a slice of white bread doesn't taste sweet or look like table sugar. Nonetheless, it's mainly made from refined wheat flour which is another simple carb, so it triggers the same sort of 'spike' in your blood sugar.

Just to confuse the issue, manufacturers add various sugars to lots of foods that you might not think of as 'sugary'. For example, lots of processed foods contain something called high fructose corn syrup or HFCS. This is a very concentrated form of sugar.

To sum up: simple carbs (including the sugar that makes things taste sweet) put your body into Fat Gain mode. Simple carbs can be hard to avoid because they are disguised under various names.

Let me just repeat that this is a *very* simplified account. I'm just giving you what you need to know to lose weight. If you want more details you can find them online or consult the relevant section on my website: www.theaddictionfixer.com .

We've now looked at The Information Problem and The Refined Carbs Problem. Let's look at the third and final problem. Then we'll see how to *solve* all the problems in an easy-ish way.

(3) The Awful Western Diet Problem

When experts refer to 'the Western Diet', they mean the kind of diet found throughout industrialised, 'First World' countries. It's a diet that includes a lot of processed and convenience food. I expect most people who read this book will be familiar with this diet.

The Western diet is awful. It's unhealthy in every way it could be. The consistently brilliant writer Michael Pollan sums it up very well:

> "People eating a Western diet are prone to a complex of chronic diseases that seldom strike people eating more traditional diets. Scientists can argue all they want about the biological mechanisms behind this phenomenon, but whichever it is, the solution to the problem would appear to remain very much the same: stop eating a Western diet."

[*Source: 'In Defense Of Food', Michael Pollan, Penguin paperback edition, copyright 2008. Part III, Section 1, pg. 140.*]

There are many things wrong with the Western diet. We've seen one of them: it involves a lot of sugar and simple carbs that put your body into Fat Gain mode. Let's look at a few of the other problems.

Separation Of Food From Nutrition

Back when we all lived in caves, food was about nutrition and survival. These days, we've lost that connection. If you eat a typical Western diet, you probably do a great deal of eating that has *nothing at all to do with nutrition*.

You eat just because you fancy a snack, or you're bored, or because it's a social occasion, or because you've fallen in love and you're sharing a tub of ice cream while you watch a movie together. You also eat to cheer yourself up (which is what the 'The Want Fix' was all about). What's more, these bad habits become self-fuelling: junk food doesn't achieve much except stimulating a desire for *more* junk food.

Using Food To Celebrate (Too Often)

It's not just negative feelings that can lead to overeating. Sometimes, *good* moods can also cause problems. Whenever we celebrate something, it's traditional in the Western diet to eat and drink unhealthy things. The general formula involves sugar, starch, fat and alcohol. Cake, for example, is mostly sugar and fat blended together.

To make things worse, you probably go into 'celebration' mode far too often. If you genuinely only ate 'fun' food on a few special occasions a year, it probably wouldn't matter. Unfortunately, overweight people have a talent for finding something to 'celebrate' every week or even every day! During my fat years, I developed a truly outstanding talent for inventing celebrations. I'm not saying I ever treated myself to a cake because someone I knew had a birthday this year, but I wasn't far off.

Food That's Nutritionally Depleted

Another problem with the Western diet is that we're accustomed to food being processed, packaged, preserved and convenient. Want something to eat? It's easy: open a tin, open a packet, heat the tray in the microwave and so on.

Unfortunately, all this convenience comes at a price. Creating convenience food involves adding preservatives, emulsifiers, stabilisers and other chemical junk so that it can travel a long way, sit on shelves for ages, be stored at home for a while and still be edible. The manufacturers also add more chemical gloop to improve the flavour, texture or colour.

It may still be 'food' in the strict sense of the word, and it's certainly fast, cheap and convenient. The bad news is that it's also nutritionally depleted and full of stuff that puts your body into Fat Gain mode.

Brainwashed Since Birth

Here's the last problem with the Western diet: it involves being brainwashed from birth. Why do you eat a lot of food that is nutritionally on a par with cardboard and makes you fat? Because you've been conditioned to do so.

Every day, you're surrounded by advertising that makes junk food seem *really* desirable. The same message is repeated over and over again: 'Hey you! Put some cheap rubbish into your body now!'. This works out just fine for the people running companies that make junk and convenience food. Fat profits (pun intended) mean they get to be wealthy, live in nice homes, enjoy several holidays every year and so on. Your money becomes their fortune.

It doesn't work out quite so well for you, the consumer. As well as paying for what is basically junk, you end up fat and with a significantly greater risk of suffering from a stroke, heart attack or various forms of cancer. Does this really sound a good deal to you?

It's weird that all this advertising works so well. Suppose you saw a big poster tomorrow and it said, "We command you to eat this rubbish that makes you fat and ruins your health so *we* can get rich at your expense!" It wouldn't be quite so appealing, would it? Yet if they just change the words, and add photos of smiling professional models, it somehow works on millions of people every day.

(Having said that, I do not regard companies that that sell junk food, confectionery or sugary drinks as the enemy. For details, see Part 2: 'Why Fast Food Companies Are Not The Enemy'.)

Progress Check

You are reading Step 3 of The Rowland Reset, which is called 'Find Your Food'. We've looked at three related problems:

- The information problem.

- The refined carbs problem.

- The awful Western diet problem.

Having looked at the problems, now it's time for the answer.

Food Fix 1: Forget About 'Going On A Diet'

So, you have a bad relationship with food and you've ended up overweight or obese. How do you put all this right?

At this point, you might think I'm going to tell you go on a diet, such as Atkins, PALEO, keto, Ringo, bongo, low carb, high carb, combine your food, separate your food, never eat food and so on.

I'm not going to do this because it would be absurd and bound to fail. Going on a diet is not a sustainable solution (unless you intend to go on a diet for the rest of your life). It's also not a solution tailored to suit your tastes and lifestyle. It can never be said too often: 'going on a diet' doesn't work.

As well as not suggesting you go on a diet, I'm also not going to tell you what to eat. I don't know what you like and I also don't know what sort of food is available in the stores and markets in your area. Even if I tried to tell you what to eat, there might be a slight language barrier. What my American and Australian friends call an 'eggplant' we Brits call an 'aubergine'. There are lots of similar examples: zucchini / courgette; squash / marrow; cilantro / coriander.

So, what's the way forward? Answer: build a new relationship with food.

Food Fix 2: Change What You Want

Start by deciding to want some new things that it makes sense to want:

1. I want to eat when I feel hungry and stop when I've had enough.

2. I want to reconnect eating *primarily* with nutrition and reduce how often I eat for other reasons (mood, habit, fun).

3. I want to avoid the simple, refined carbs that trigger Fat Gain mode, especially sugar and anything that tastes sweet.

You can transform your mind so you want these things by using the Want Fix.

Meditate and communicate with your Fixer. Say that these new choices are the *real* way to make you happy and keep you feeling good. Explain that they will help you to lose weight and build a good, new relationship with food that is much more likely to lead to sustained good health. Ask your Fixer to do its job using these new methods.

Food Fix 3: Go On Your Food Adventure

Next step: I invite you to go on a big, exciting adventure. Your mission is to find every kind of fresh produce that you like.

This is easy to do. Explore all the sources of food you have near you, from big supermarkets to smaller shops and stores. The only ones that count are the ones you can get to fairly easily and on a regular basis.

Go For Green

Start by exploring the fresh produce section, especially anything green, and in particular anything green and leafy. Keep an open mind, try stuff you've never tried before, see what works for you.

All vegetables and fresh produce items are fairly easy to prepare. Most of the time you just need to boil veg in a pan of water, or use a steamer, until it's edible. If there's anything you don't know how to prepare, and you can't ask anyone, go online and search for the answer. You'll always find an article or a video explaining what to do.

This is an adventure, so enjoy it. You will discover some things you don't like. You will discover others that, to your surprise, you *do* like. Give it all a fair chance. You can't take one mouthful of something and say "I hate it!" Allow yourself time to get used to it.

Why focus on vegetables and fresh produce? Because they are all superfoods. No sugar, no added chemicals, satisfying, full of vitamins and minerals, good fibre. They also contain a more protein than most people realise. If you ever doubt this, remember that all gorillas are vegetarians. (Don't ever get this the wrong way round and say all vegetarians are gorillas. The rumour that I once made this mistake during a public talk is entirely false and it never happened, okay?)

Complex Carbs

You're on your big, exciting food adventure. You've found some green stuff, especially leafy green stuff, that you like.

You're going to need some carbohydrates. The trick here is to choose complex carbs that your body has to work harder to break down and digest. The prefix 'whole—' is a good one to look out for. Wholegrain rice, wholewheat pasta... stuff like that. Legumes are good (beans, chickpeas, lentils), and so are barley, quinoa, potatoes and similar foods. You can search online for 'examples of complex carbs'.

Take the same basic approach as you did for greens: keep an open mind, take stuff home, try it and find what you like.

Be on your guard for deception. Some manufacturers label stuff as if it's healthier than it really is. They might slap the 'whole' prefix on foods that aren't actually that wholesome. Be careful and check stuff out as far as you can (the internet is a great source of information). You know the difference between simple carbs (poison) and complex carbs (good). Aim for the complex ones that release their energy *slowly*.

Protein

You're going to need some sources of protein.

If you're a carnivore, then meat and fish are two obvious choices. There are many others worth exploring. Beans and pulses are good sources of protein and (as I've already mentioned) you can get plenty of good protein from the green stuff and plant sources that you've already checked out.

There are many vegetarian/vegan options too, such as tofu and tempeh, and some 'meat substitutes' that have various branded names. We have one in the UK called Quorn. It's basically a form of mushroom protein but they make it look and taste a bit like meat. I found I quite like it, although these days I don't eat much of it. There will probably be equivalents in your shops and stores.

Eggs and some dairy products such as cottage cheese are also good for protein, although of course they won't interest you if you prefer to avoid dairy products. My advice is the same: explore with an open mind, try stuff, see if you like it.

Fats

Finally, you're going to need some sources of fat. As you know, if you want to lose weight, fat is not the enemy. Sugar and simple carbs are the enemy. Fat is not only an essential part of your diet but also a very enjoyable one since it tends to make things taste nice.

If you eat meat, that's one good source of fat. Plant-based whole foods that are sources of fibre, minerals and protein, like nuts and seeds, are also sources of unsaturated fats and omega oils. Try to choose unsaturated fats rather than saturated. You can read about the difference online if you really want to but it soon starts to sound like a really boring chemistry lesson. (Is there any other kind of chemistry lesson?)

Get Into Labels

Start focusing on food that doesn't *need* an ingredients label because it's just fresh produce.

If you do buy anything that has an ingredients label, study it and make smart choices. Even if you do nothing else, look at the carbs and sugars. You want this to be a really *low* percentage of whatever you're buying. Anything higher than 5% just isn't worth it.

If you can see High Fructose Corn Syrup (HFCS) on the label, don't even *think* of eating it. It's a very concentrated form of sugar. In terms of how good it is for you, the letters might as well stand for 'Highly Fattening: Contains Sewage'.

In his superb book 'The Obesity Code', Jason Fung provides a long list of names that manufacturers use to disguise the sugar content of food. These include 'hydrolysed starch', 'corn sweetener', 'palm syrup' and 'agave nectar'. As he points out, sly manufacturers often use several different names for sugar on one label so that the total gets broken down into several smaller percentages. This means the word 'sugar' doesn't appear top of the ingredients list. Don't fall for these tricks.

The Adventure That Never Ends

Go on your big food adventure. Slowly but surely, build up your list of healthy foods you actually like and enjoy.

Put together meals from the veg, complex carbs, protein and fat that you've found you like. Base most of your diet on whole foods and plants, especially leafy green stuff. Add some sources of protein (and try stuff other than just meat or fish). Add complex carbs that won't trigger blood sugar spikes.

Kiss goodbye to the Western diet that is slowly killing you. Wave farewell to the brainwashing and advertising. Stop relying on processed food, ready meals and junk that's basically just fat and sugar. Start avoiding packaged food that comes with a long list of ingredients featuring preservatives, emulsifiers, flavourings, whatever was lying around on the factory floor during the late shift and who knows what else.

Reconnect the idea of eating with nutrition and stop eating for other reasons (mood, habit, fun). Eat when you feel hungry, stop when you've had enough.

Keep learning, keep discovering.

These days, there are 'meal in a box' companies that deliver a set of ingredients and a recipe for you to follow. If you like the sound of this, try one or two of these companies and see if you like them. They may have ideas and suggestions you wouldn't have thought of, plus it's fun to invite a friend over and prepare the meal together. The more hopeless you think you are as a chef, the more fun it tends to be!

If you want to learn more about good food choices, have a look online. It only takes a few seconds to search for terms like these:

- 'List of complex carbs'.

- 'What are whole foods?'

- 'Examples of legumes'.

- 'Ways to cook and prepare broccoli'.

- 'Alternatives to meat and fish'.

Have fun finding out whatever you need to know!

I want to take a moment to clarify one point. I'm not saying that you will never again eat for fun or tuck into some pizza or chocolate cake. The point is to get to the stage where:

- You aren't addicted to sugar or anything else.

- You *mostly* eat in a way that's enjoyable and healthy.

- You can (if you want) occasionally enjoy 'fun' food in a way that doesn't have any bad consequences.

This is a very nice stage to get to. Once in a while if I really feel like it I indulge in some fun food or tuck into a pizza. However, these days I can do so in a way that doesn't lead to any problems. I'm not addicted to anything, my weight and fitness are good and if I put on a bit of weight I can quickly and easily get rid of it again.

A Bit More Shopping Time?

One consequence of choosing fresh food rather than convenience junk is that you might not be able to shop for food just once a week. You may have to go for groceries two or three times a week.

Don't use this as an excuse to avoid building a better relationship with food. You can do it. The total time you spend shopping doesn't increase by much. You're just dividing it into two or three visits. It's a small price to pay for this great change in your life.

Don't Miss Examples Under Your Own Nose!

During this process of rebuilding your relationship with food, keep your eyes and ears open. Pay attention to what other people eat, especially if they seem fit and healthy. Look at friends, neighbours, co-workers and see if you can't learn a thing or two.

Here are two examples from my own adventure.

During one chapter of my life, I had a wonderful girlfriend who loved nothing more than to cook some pasta and add pesto. At the time, given my limitless ignorance about food, I didn't really know what pesto was. I thought it *looked* a bit slimy which, to be fair, it sometimes does. As a result, I never once felt curious enough to even try it. Many years later, when I went on my weight loss journey, I discovered that I absolutely *love* pesto! These days I use it all the time and not just with pasta (although 'pasta and pesto' does sound rather poetically meant-to-be). If I'd just been a bit more open-minded during that earlier part of my life, I would have discovered the pleasure of pesto much sooner.

It's the same story with hummus. Many years ago, I shared a house with someone who absolutely loved hummus and used it all the time. I didn't know what it was and never bothered to try it. When I started losing weight and exploring different foods, I made the very happy discovery that I *really* like hummus. There are several different varieties and I've yet to meet one I don't like! I wish I'd made this discovery much sooner.

I'm sharing these stories just to illustrate the point: when you keep an open mind and try different things you'll make interesting discoveries.

Food Fix 4: Find Your FANG

The fourth and final step, in terms of fixing your relationship with food, is to find your FANG: your own personal Food And Nutrition Genius.

Think of all the people you know who have access to the same shops and stores as you. Find someone who isn't overweight and seems to eat in a healthy way. Ask them to help you improve your relationship with food, including advice about what to try and what to avoid.

Your FANG's role is not to tell you what to eat. Their role is to encourage you, suggest stuff you might like and maybe answer questions about how to prepare certain foods or add a bit of extra flavour to them. Ask your FANG if you can go food shopping with them once or twice to learn about some of the choices they make. Anyone who has a good relationship with food will *love* helping you to improve yours.

If you can't find your FANG in real life, you can definitely find one online. All that matters is that they are in the same part of the world as you, so you have access to the same choices and use the same vocabulary. Finding a FANG isn't essential to fix your relationship with food but it does make your weight loss journey more enjoyable.

The best FANG I know is my friend Sal Dhalla, who is known as The Food Witch. Sal knows more about the simple joy of good food than anyone else I know. She's based in London but of course, thanks to the internet, she's next door to everywhere. You can find her online. If you want to improve your relationship with food, contact Sal and learn as much as you can from her. She's smart, fun, cool, very knowledgeable, passionate about her work and great to know.

What Will Happen?

When you follow my Food Fix suggestions, here's what will happen.

If you had an addiction to sugar and starch, you will go through a 'sugar crash' as your body adjusts to not being flooded with easy sugar all the time. This typically lasts a couple of days, during which you may feel a bit lacking in energy and want to occasionally take a nap. Don't worry. After this brief 'sugar crash', your energy levels will stabilise and you'll be free from your addiction forever.

You will have a very happy, healthy and enjoyable relationship with food. There will be occasions when you choose to enjoy 'fun' food and favourite treats, but you won't be addicted to anything and you'll know how to do this in a way that doesn't have any bad consequences.

You'll discover some new foods you enjoy. Your palette will improve and you'll start actually tasting your food properly, rather than saturating your taste buds with sugar all the time. You will lose weight, because you know how to put your body into Fat Loss mode and keep it there. You'll lose weight quite rapidly at first and then it will slow down to a steadier, more gradual rate that's less dramatic but still satisfying.

You will save money, because fresh produce and green veg cost a lot less than highly packaged and processed food. You'll also notice that you have a lot less waste and packaging to throw away.

That's what will happen when you use the Food Fix. I'm going to end Step 3 here. However, if you want additional advice, see Part 2: 'More About Finding Your Food'.

Progress Check

Here's the story so far.

Step 1: 'The Basic Question'.

Step 2: 'Change Your Mind'.

We've just finished Step 3: 'Find Your Food'. We looked at general principles for building a positive relationship with food so you can lose as much weight as you want.

If you want some additional information, see Part 2: 'More About Finding Your Food'.

The next step is all about exercise. Don't panic — I am *not* going to suggest you go to the gym!

Step 4: Find Your Exercise

Surprising as it may seem, exercise is *not* a good way to lose weight. Back when we all lived in caves, food was sometimes scarce. As a result, we evolved to be very good at storing food on our bodies (as fat) and making it last as long as possible. To put this in scientific terms: evolution hates people who are trying to lose weight.

Overweight people are often advised to do lots of exercise in an effort to 'burn off' some body fat. This type of misguided advice is part of the information problem I talked about earlier. The fact is, you can do a *lot* of physical work and only use up a small amount of fat. If you went on a vigorous cross-country run tomorrow — assuming you could manage this level of exertion — you would lose very little weight. You would feel you had invested a lot of effort for very little reward.

Losing weight is *mostly* about changing your relationship with food, as we've seen in Step 3: 'Find Your Food'. So, here's the picture:

Diet: mostly about losing weight + helps a bit with fitness.

Exercise: mostly about fitness +helps a bit with losing weight.

Even though exercise only helps a *bit* with weight loss, there are lots of good reasons to start exercising regularly:

- There are lots of health benefits.

- It's the perfect antidote to stress.

- Fitness feels great and the journey from fat to fit is an *amazing* experience.

- It makes sense to work on diet and exercise at the same time.

There's a much longer and more detailed list of benefits in Part 2: 'More About Benefits'.

Okay, so how do you start exercising? Race down to the nearest gym and sign up with breathless excitement? No. For most people reading this book, this would not be a great idea. Turn the page...

Go On Your Exercise Adventure

In Step 3, 'Find Your Food', I suggested you go on a big food adventure: keep an open mind, explore Fat Loss foods and find the stuff you like.

I'm going to make the same suggestion when it comes to exercise. Keep an open mind, explore your options and find a form of exercise that's right for you.

What counts as exercise? Well, in technical terms it's defined as anything that gets your heartbeat up to about two thirds of your theoretical maximum for at least twenty minutes. Your 'theoretical maximum' will of course vary depending on your age, sex and what sort of condition you're in. And whether or not you're a horse.

A simpler way to define exercise is this: anything that, when you first try it, raises your heartbeat significantly, leaving you a bit out of breath and feeling you can't do it for very long.

There are basically two types of exercise: aerobic and anaerobic. Aerobic is the sort of exercise that gets your heart and lungs (your cardiovascular system) working hard for a sustained period of time, such as jogging, cycling or swimming. Anaerobic exercise doesn't involve the same kind of sustained cardiovascular effort. The commonest example is lifting weights. This involves expending energy in short, concentrated bursts rather than continuously over a period of time.

For weight loss and fitness, some type of aerobic exercise is probably best (although if you want to start lifting weights I'm not going to say you can't). Of course, you could do *both*. Just to keep things simple, in this section I'll assume you're only going to take up *one* form of exercise, at least initially.

So, you're going to go on an adventure, like you did with food, and find a form of exercise you actually like. There are countless different options to choose from. Let's look at some possibilities.

Lots And Lots Of Choices

When you start looking for a form of exercise that's right for you, there are plenty of options to consider. You *can* join a gym if that's what you feel you really want to do. However, there are countless alternatives. Here are just a few:

Swimming. Cycling. Rowing. Squash. Tennis. Badminton.

Team sports, perhaps in an amateur or 'Sunday' league.

Martial arts. Karate, Kung Fu, Aikido... there are many different types of martial arts to explore and they always give beginners a warm welcome.

Jogging indoors on a running machine. Jogging in parks or across natural terrain and countryside. Jogging in an urban environment.

Joining an indoor or outdoor exercise class led by an instructor (such an 'Exercise in the park' group).

Aerobics. Calisthenics. Boxercise. Kettlebell exercises.

Introductory gymnastic classes. Any other sort of class that involves physical exercise.

Track and field disciplines.

Obviously, cultural factors affect which options are available to you. There will be some sports and forms of exercise that are particularly popular in your part of the world, making it easy to find the appropriate facilities. It's easy to take up ice hockey in Canada, netball in New Zealand and — I am not making this up — oil wrestling in Turkey.

Even when people talk about 'going to the gym', that one phrase covers quite a broad range of entirely different options. Some people go to the gym mainly to do cardiovascular exercises or 'cardio' for short, such as using the running, cycling or rowing machines. Others focus on strength training, using either free weights (like barbells) or resistance machines. Another option is to attend specific classes, such as a strength training or 'spin' class (a workout using an exercise bike). Some gyms have swimming pools and offer classes like water aerobics.

That's quite a wide range of options already, but there's more. You see, you don't just get to choose which form of exercise feels right for you. In addition, you also get to choose *how* you pursue it.

You choose **who's involved**. You can just exercise on your own if that's what you prefer. Alternatively, you can pair up with a friend and go exercising together, or join a club that does whatever it is you want to do (such as a swimming or martial arts club).

You choose **the time of day**. You can exercise first thing in the morning, at lunchtime, in the evening or at some other time. Different people have different preferences and of course it depends what you can fit in with your daily home or work routine.

You choose how much **consistency** you want. You might want to always exercise at the same time, or have a set of times, or forget about a schedule and just enjoy your exercise whenever it suits you.

You choose how much **repetition** is involved. Do you always cycle around the exact, same route, or have a few different ones, or make it up as you go along? Do you follow a set workout at the gym or just improvise your way through it? It's your choice. Some people like to do the same thing every time. Others prefer to build plenty of variety into their exercise or just 'freestyle' and do whatever they feel like at the time.

You choose the **details** about how you exercise. Take jogging as an example. You can do this on a running machine in the gym, or outdoors over natural terrain like parks and fields, or outdoors along the pavements / sidewalks in your neighbourhood.

You choose **what else you do** while you exercise. Some people like to listen to music or podcasts while they exercise. In most gyms, you can exercise while watching TV or music videos if you want. Some people just want to focus on the exercise itself with nothing else added.

When you think about all the different forms of exercise and all the options involved, you can see there are almost limitless possibilities. If you try a form of exercise and it's not quite right for you, maybe you just need to make a few small changes. I found I did *not* like jogging across natural terrain (too uneven and irregular for me) but *love* jogging along streets and pavements.

All you have to do is go on your adventure, keep an open mind and find the type of regular exercise that's right for you. Ask friends and neighbours what *they* do to get regular exercise. Maybe your local council or authority has information on their website about exercise, fitness and sport facilities.

If you happen to find two or three ways of exercising that you like, great! This will provide a bit more variety so you're exercising different muscle groups during different exercise sessions, which is a good idea.

Walking And Yoga

Going for walks is better than nothing but, unfortunately, doesn't really count as exercise for the purpose of losing weight and getting fit. It just doesn't make your heart and lungs work hard enough to deliver the benefits I've mentioned and to help you achieve fitness.

The same goes for yoga. Yoga is great and has much to recommend it, but it's not sufficiently intensive, in cardiovascular terms, to count as exercise the way I'm talking about it in this book. It has lots of benefits but does not, in and of itself, help you to get fit.

If walking and yoga are your only options, then by all means choose them. Just be aware that they won't produce the same benefits as forms of exercise that ask your heart and lungs to work a little harder.

What If You Don't Like Any Exercise?

What if you were to say to me that you've tried every form of exercise under the sun and you don't like any of them?

I'd find this hard to believe. There are very few people who can't find *any* form of exercise they enjoy. I would suspect that you are experiencing *emotional* resistance to the notion of exercise. Luckily, there are ways of dealing with this. See Part 2, 'Overcoming Emotional Resistance'.

You might also want to read the very long list of benefits in Part 2: 'More About Benefits'. It's a pretty long list of benefits and they're all yours for the asking. Perhaps the list will encourage you to go over your exercise options one more time and find something you like.

For thirty years, I was a completely sedentary, zero-exercise human sloth. Exercise was my kryptonite. I wanted to exercise like I wanted to lick a wrestler's armpit. At the age of 56, when I weighed 116 kg (256 pounds), I found a form of exercise I liked. In my case, to my great surprise, this turned out to be jogging. If I could find a form of exercise I like, I'm confident you can do it too.

If you're adamant that you've tried every option, from cycling to a twice-weekly Boxercise class, from rhythmic gymnastics to competitive nude volleyball, and you can honestly say you can't stand *any* of them, you're the first person I've ever met who could truthfully say this. You can still lose weight just by mending your relationship with food, as described in Step 3, 'Find Your Food'. It will take a bit longer and you won't get fit, but you can still do it.

Four Principles Of Exercise

Let's say you've got to the point where you've explored a few options and found a form of exercise you actually enjoy. There are four key principles you need to know about.

Principle 1: DDJ

The first one is DDJ, which stands for:

Discover, Don't Judge

When you start taking regular exercise, don't set yourself a target or think you have to achieve a certain standard of performance. Instead, just try your best, discover what happens and see what you can do.

When I started jogging, I didn't set myself a target. I just set off to find out how long I could keep going for. The answer turned out to be about ninety seconds, after which I was completely exhausted! I had to stop and walk the rest of the route I had worked out. You might think this sounds rather pathetic but I didn't think of it that way. I hadn't set myself a target so there was no sense of success or failure. I was just discovering what I could do.

Whatever form of exercise you choose, it's important to adopt this same attitude. There is no target. You are just *discovering* what you can do, and whatever you discover is perfectly good. You can work out a route, distance, challenge or set of exercises you want to work towards and complete *eventually*. However, for each individual session, always DDJ.

This is important for a few reasons. First of all, it avoids any negative feelings. This is a crucial aspect of getting fit and staying fit. I'll explain more in the next section, Step 5, 'Staying Great'.

Secondly, when you're starting out, targets are irrelevant. There is no standard you need to achieve. As the saying goes, you are still way ahead of everyone who isn't even trying.

When you're beginning the process of losing weight and getting fit, it doesn't matter what you can or cannot do. What matters is that you make a start. Nobody is going to criticise you or sneer. Even if they do — which they won't — you are immune from all criticism. "Yes, I'm unfit and out of shape. So what? I'm doing something positive about it. I'm proud of this. Do you have any better ideas?"

When you start: Discover, Don't Judge.

Principle 2: JTU

You have found a form of exercise you enjoy. You have made a start and you know about DDJ. The second key principle is JTU, which stands for:

Just Turn Up

One great joy of getting fit is that you never, ever need to *try* to improve. The improvement just happens automatically, like magic. All you have to do is keep turning up and enjoying your sure, steady and certain improvement. It's a wonderful thing to experience.

Maybe the first time you try to exercise, you'll be able to do very little (like when I found I could only jog for about ninety seconds). This doesn't matter. The next time, you'll make a small improvement. Little by little, you'll get better and better. The gradual improvement is certain and automatic. All you have to do is find some exercise you enjoy and then JTU.

Principle 3: FOAM

The third key principle is FOAM, which stands for:

Focus On 'After' Mood

On rare occasions, I know that I ought to go for a run but I don't feel I'm in the right mood. There could be any number of interesting reasons for this. Feelings and emotions are, by definition, not always easy to understand.

If you're ever in this position, here's what I suggest: focus on how you will feel *after* the exercise rather than how you feel *now*. In other words, focus on the 'after' mood, not the 'before' mood.

After you've done your exercise, you'll feel great. You will be justifiably proud of yourself for having done the exercise you had planned to do. In addition, you will be full of nice, warm tingles all over, and you will have lots of your body's natural 'happy' hormones, called endorphins, flowing through your bloodstream. You'll feel the warming, exercise 'after glow'. It's worth it. You're worth it.

Tip: when you have a really great exercise session, and feel fantastic, take a moment to enjoy the feeling and save it in your bank of sense memories. Use this memory next time you need to focus on your after mood.

Principle 4: MIDIM

Key Principle 4 is MIDIM, which stands for:

Minor Differences Matter

Earlier in this section, I listed some of the choices you can make when you're finding the type of exercise that's right for you (who's involved / time of day / degree of consistency and so on).

Just a few small changes here and there can transform how you feel about any particular option. You might hate doing a workout on your own but love it when you join a class (or vice versa). You might hate cycling if you stick to a rigid schedule but love it if you go a bit more 'freestyle'.

This is a really important point that doesn't get mentioned enough. It doesn't make sense to say something like, "I don't like swimming". This makes it sound as if 'swimming' is just one, fixed option, and everyone who enjoys swimming does it the exact same way. This is nonsense.

Consider two examples. John goes swimming on his own, always first thing in the morning, on the same days each week and enters local competitions as often as possible. Jane goes with a friend to swimming classes at different times each week and couldn't care less about competitions. Same basic choice (swimming) but enjoyed in very different ways.

Keep an open mind, try different things and discover what works best for you. Always remember that minor differences matter. If you think you don't like a particular option, see if one or two minor differences change you how you feel about it.

Putting this another way, I sometimes say 'small differences make a big difference', which sounds crazy but I think conveys what I mean.

This concludes the four principles I wanted to share:

- DDJ. Discover, don't judge.

- JTU. Just turn up.

- FOAM. Focus on 'after' mood.

- MIDIM. Minor differences matter.

Some Final Notes On Exercise

How Often Should You Exercise?

Only you can decide this for yourself. As a general rule, my advice would be to exercise as often as you feel like it — but avoid the extremes of too little or too much.

If you're only exercising once a week, there's something wrong. Why would you only do something once a week if you like it and enjoy it? This suggests you haven't found a type of exercise you really like. Remember the MIDIM principle: Minor Differences Matter. You may find you only have to make *minor* changes to how you exercise to start enjoying it more. For example, I found I do not like jogging across fields and natural terrain (despite my love of nature) but much prefer an urban environment.

On the other hand, don't exercise every day. Rest days matter. They are when your body recovers, carries out any repairs and grows new muscle fibres. Of course, if you use 'rest days' as an excuse to avoid exercise, you're just being dishonest with yourself.

Once you start to exercise regularly, your body will tell you how often to exercise and for how long. Listen to your body and try varying your routine until you find what works best for you.

Keep Track Of Your Progress

You need a way to keep track of your progress. Make sure you have some good bathroom scales and use them. I bought some 'Hanson HX5000' scales that have a memory feature — you can see what you weigh now *and* what you weighed last time. I've found this to be a very useful feature.

Have an official weighing day once a week. Get up, have your normal morning visit to the bathroom and then weigh yourself as near to naked as is practical / comfortable. This is how to get your 'official' weight for that week. You can weigh yourself more often if you're curious, but don't get obsessive about it. Also, remember that only the week-to-week numbers are really going to give you an accurate picture. Daily measurements can fluctuate wildly for all sorts of reasons.

Ignore gimmicky scales that say they can tell you other things like your body mass index, percentage fat, star sign divided by your age in weeks and similar nonsense. They are not reliable and can be misleading.

How Long Will It Take?

On the subject of progress, you might find yourself wondering, "How long will it take to achieve all my weight and fitness goals?"

Here's the answer: the sooner you start, the sooner you'll get there. Rather than wondering how long it will take, just remind yourself that you will certainly achieve all your goals. All you have to do is follow the Rowland Reset and JTU. You will lose fat far more quickly than you gained it but the time is takes isn't really important. When you're on the right road to your destination, it's still the right road whether you move along it slowly or quickly.

The right path is still the right path, whether you walk or run.

This is also worth noting:

'It takes time' is not the same as 'it's difficult'.

Never feel negative about a plan just because it's going to take a while. Enjoy the fact that you know what to do, you're going to do it and you'll reach your goals. There's a longer section about this in Part Two.

Don't Think You Can Buy Fitness

Please don't make the mistake of thinking that *buying* things means *making progress*. It doesn't. Purchase is not progress. Fitness is something you achieve, not something you buy.

You don't need to spend much money to lose weight and get fit. For most forms of exercise, you just need some loose, comfortable clothing. If you need trainers or running shoes, you don't need to spend a fortune on the latest, heavily advertised 'cool' brands. Getting fit is not a fashion parade. When I took up jogging, I just got the cheapest pair of trainers that seemed suitable for the job, based on a few online reviews, and they served me perfectly well.

Companies that want to sell you sportswear or swimwear will, of course, tell you different. So will companies selling gadgets that keep track of your pace, the distance you've covered, the amount of oxygen in your elbows, your pulse divided by your average stride and all sorts of other statistics.

Don't fall for the hype. Only buy what you need and don't pay for overhyped brands and a logo. I will intentionally repeat myself: fitness is something you achieve, not something you buy.

Stiffness, Strains And Sprains

When you work muscles that haven't worked hard in a while, some chemical changes happen that can lead to your muscles feeling stiff. This is sometimes called the 'lactic acid' problem, although this term is slightly inaccurate. All you need to know is that this problem will go away after one or two exercise sessions.

Here's another small problem. When you start exercising, you will probably have to deal with with occasional strains and sprains. Always take these seriously. Take some time off and let your body heal itself. Also, see if you need any physiotherapy or simple home exercises to help the healing process. Never use minor injuries as an excuse to avoid exercise. If you need to allow a slight sprain to heal, resting for a few days makes sense; avoiding exercise for four months doesn't. If you've found some exercise you *like*, and you're honest with yourself, this shouldn't be a problem.

I can't make this book into a complete guide to safe, responsible ways to exercise. This would be impossible since a hundred readers (assuming I ever get that many) might exercise in a hundred different ways. All I can say is, whatever exercise you choose, do it safely and responsibly so you minimise strains, sprains and other unwanted consequences. Take good advice and stay free from injury.

The point is to exercise safely and without injuries or other unwanted ill effects. The longer you carry on exercising, the easier this becomes.

Progress Check

Step 1: 'The Basic Question'.

Step 2: 'Change Your Mind' using the Want Fix.

Step 3: 'Find Your Food'.

You've just finished Step 4: 'Find Your Exercise'. I suggested you go on an adventure to find the right sort of exercise for you and mentioned four useful principles (DDJ and so on).

I've included some additional information in Part 2: 'More About Finding Your Exercise'.

What's next? Losing weight and getting fit is great. However, there's no point in doing this unless you also know how to *stay* great. This is the subject of the fifth and final step.

Step 5: Stay Great

I hope that, armed with the information in this book, you manage to lose weight and get fit the easy-ish way.

However, this isn't the end of the story. It's one thing to *get* fit and healthy. It's quite another to *stay* that way. In this fifth and final step, I want to offer you some suggestions about how to do this.

Stay Positive (As Far As Possible)

Maintaining a positive outlook on life is a profoundly important part of staying great and not putting the weight back on. Let me explain why.

If you have negotiated successfully with your Fixer, it will try to keep you feeling good using the new, positive and non-fattening methods you have suggested. Most of the time, this should work pretty well. However, if you spur your Fixer into action very often, this can lead to a couple of problems.

First problem: as you know, if someone is overworked they are more likely to make mistakes. Your Fixer is no exception. The more often it has to do its job, the greater the chance of it making a mistake — such as using Fat Gain foods to cheer you up.

Second problem: if your Fixer gets triggered a lot, it might conclude that the new methods you have asked it to use aren't working very well. As a result, it might lose faith in these new methods and go back to the old ones.

For these reasons, *you want to give your Fixer as little work to do as possible*. Since your Fixer springs into action whenever you feel any negative emotion, it's a good idea to have as few negative thoughts and feelings as possible. In short:

- Negativity leads back to fat (or at least increases the risk).

- Positivity leads forward to fit.

Obviously, unless you live a very strange life, you can't feel positive about everything, all the time. Life has its annoyances and frustrations — there's a wasp for every picnic, so to speak. The point is to *try* to stay as positive as you can, as often as you can, to give your Fixer as little work to do as possible. One thing that will help a great deal is to use positive language.

Positive Language

You can't control everything in life and bad stuff happens. What you *can* control is the language you use and how you express yourself. In order to stay great and not put the weight back on, I strongly recommend that you start expressing yourself in positive terms.

It's not hard to get the hang of doing this. You just have to think about things in a slightly different way. This applies to your thoughts and *internal* monologue as well as whatever you say to other people. For example, don't refer to yourself in a negative way. Be a good friend to yourself and always look for the positive spin. Here are some examples.

Negative: "I'm hopeless at this."

Positive: "I might not be great at this yet, but I'm doing my best to learn and getting better all the time."

Negative: "I really messed that up."

Positive: "I tried my best but I was unlucky. It was a difficult situation and didn't turn out the way I'd hoped. We all know life has its ups and downs and not every day is a trophy day. I'll learn from this and do better next time."

You get the idea? Of course, it's important to accept responsibility for yourself and your actions. Nonetheless, you can learn to be less self-critical and more forgiving. Go easy on the self-blame and learn the art of accepting yourself, respecting yourself, and referring to yourself in a positive way.

It's particularly important to express yourself in a positive way regarding your weight and fitness journey. For example:

Negative: "Oh no... my weight's actually gone *up* a bit! That's totally unfair. I did everything right last week and it just doesn't make sense!"

Positive: "My weight has actually gone up a bit. It's a bit puzzling, I suppose, but no problem. I wonder if I can learn anything from this? I expect next week will be better so I'll look forward to that."

During my weight loss journey, if I ever found my weight had gone up a bit, in a seemingly inexplicable way, I tried not to react negatively. I just shrugged, hummed the theme from 'The Twilight Zone' and wrote it off as one of life's big, beautiful mysteries.

The Plateau Effect

As regards staying positive, it's important to know about what's called the Plateau Effect. You might think that when you lose weight, you'll see a steady, consistent reduction, like the chart shown on the left. In reality, even when you do everything right, your progress is more likely to resemble the chart on the right. Sometimes you'll lose more weight than you expected, sometimes less. Occasionally, your weight might even go *up* slightly (although that's quite rare).

What is certain is that you will occasionally experience a *plateau*: a period when your progress becomes a flat line, neither up nor down, and seems to be stuck that way. This can last up to about ten days.

There are two ways to deal with a plateau. The first way is to sulk, stomp around the house and yell, "It's so unfair! I've done everything right but my weight just *won't* move!" Then you can spend the rest of the day gorging on chocolate in protest. This response is not recommended.

The slightly preferable response involves two steps.

(1) Shrug, smile, stay positive. Say to yourself, "It doesn't matter. Weight loss is a bit of a weird process and sometimes it just doesn't seem to make sense."

(2) Realise that every plateau has both a beginning and an end. The plateau may be puzzling and a bit annoying but it will end eventually. If you're doing everything right, you will lose weight and achieve your targets. An occasional plateau doesn't make any difference.

What's more, it is often the case that a plateau is followed by a phase where your rate of progress *speeds up* a bit. In other words, a disappointing week or two tends to be followed by weeks when you'll be really *delighted* with your progress. I can't promise that this will happen every single time, but it does happen pretty often.

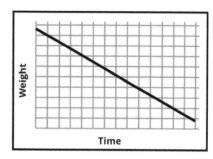
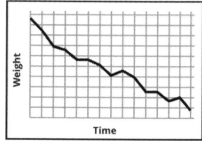

How Much Weight Should You Lose?

Only you can decide for yourself how much weight you want to lose. However, let me offer you a suggestion. Go online and find a Body Mass Index (BMI) calculator. When you enter a few details about yourself, this will show your healthy weight range (between being underweight and overweight). Whatever this range happens to be, divide it by three and look at the middle third. Choose a convenient, round number within this range and let this be your target weight.

There's no science behind this and of course you can lose less weight or more as you prefer. It's just a suggestion that avoids being either too ambitious or not ambitious enough. Trying to get your weight all the way down to the bottom end of your healthy weight range might feel too daunting and ambitious. Getting it down to *just* inside the top end of this range probably isn't ambitious enough — you will find it very easy to stray back into the overweight zone.

Once you have achieved your ideal weight, stick to it. Let this be 'the new normal' for you. Once in a rare while, if you want to enjoy a special occasion or be a bit indulgent, you can eat and drink whatever you like *so long as you don't go back into the 'overweight' zone*. Having enjoyed this rare, special occasion, get back to your ideal weight before you have any more special events or indulgent occasions.

Some 'experts' and books place far too much emphasis on the BMI Index. Please don't make this mistake. It's not a very precise tool and there are many factors that it fails to take into account. However, it's useful as a quick way to figure out what you want your weight to be and therefore how much weight you want to lose.

I started off at 116 kg (256 pounds) and, having had a look at my healthy weight range, decided my new weight would be 76 kg (168 pounds). This is only *just* within the middle third of my healthy range but it's what felt right for me.

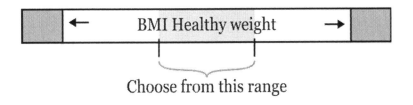

Choose from this range

No-No To 'Yo-Yo'

The notion of 'yo-yo' dieting is well known. People who go on a diet usually lose some weight for a short time. When they abandon the diet, as they always do eventually, they regain all the weight they lost and add a little extra, ending up heavier than they were in the first place. Some time later, they try again and the same thing happens.

This is unsurprising given that going on a diet is such a misguided and ineffective idea. I went through this cycle many times during my fat years. A time-lapse movie of my body shape would look like someone playing the accordion.

In this book, I am *not* suggesting you go on a diet so I doubt you'll have this 'yo-yo' problem. Nonetheless, once you have lost the weight you want to lose, *don't take it for granted* that you'll stay lean and fit. Sustain and nourish your relationship with your Fixer. It has learned new ways to keep you happy whenever necessary. Help it get used to these new strategies. Continue to talk to your Fixer and thank it when it looks after you the way you *want* to be looked after.

Every day, enjoy being free from addiction, free from your old habits and having control over your weight and fitness.

Mind And Body

After you've lost weight, and developed a new relationship with food, it might take a while for your *mind* to catch up with your *body*.

Suppose you were overweight for ten years before you used the Rowland Reset and got your weight down. For those ten years, your attitudes, behaviours and choices were those of an overweight person who regularly ate Fat Gain foods. It's understandable if your mind takes a while to absorb the changes and get used to your new way of living.

Sustaining a good relationship with your Fixer is an important part of this. In addition, recognise that this is *an ongoing process*. Give your mind time to catch up and be aware of all the choices and decisions you make. Be ready to stop yourself from time to time and say, "Ah, wait a minute. That thought or impulse I've just had is a *relic* from the old days. It's a negative pattern that doesn't really fit how I live my life now. I have better options these days and should update my ideas and behaviour accordingly."

Losing weight and getting fit isn't just about working with your body. Work with your mind as well. They come as a package!

You're Free, Not Deprived

Once you've lost weight, never succumb to the delusion that you are being *deprived* of anything or that you are no longer *allowed* to have certain foods. These are both negative feelings that can lead back to weight gain.

When someone says you can't have something, it's natural to feel resentment. This intensifies your desire to get what you've been told you can't have — especially if it's something you see lots of other people (apparently) enjoying. Any negative feelings of being deprived will prompt your Fixer to try to make sure that you, too, enjoy whatever 'treat' is being considered.

How can you avoid these feelings and problems? Well, the *words* you use can make a big difference to how you feel. Consider these two ways of expressing yourself:

(1) "I *can't have* chocolate. I'm *not allowed* to have it anymore. I have to *deny* myself that pleasure — even though I can see lots of other people enjoying it and they look perfectly okay."

(2) "I can have all the chocolate I want. The amount I want is precisely 'none' because I know that, despite the way is advertised, it isn't my friend. It's just Fat Gain junk that hurts my body and would lead to me being overweight and unfit again. I'd rather eat something I love, like some fresh greens, that won't cause a sugar spike, won't harm my body and won't lead to being overweight."

The first version is full of alarming words and phrases: 'can't have', 'not allowed', 'deny'. These are likely to trigger a sense of protest which, in turn, can lead to a sense of 'rebellion' and a desire to have something purely to demonstrate that you refuse to be imprisoned by rules.

The second option lacks any trace of this negativity. It doesn't convey any sense of denial or deprivation. You have all the choices, all the power, all the control. You choose to use your power to look after yourself. You are in control and prefer great food that *doesn't* harm you as opposed to junk that harmed you in the past and, as you know perfectly well, would do so again.

You're not a slave to foods that will hurt you. You are *free* from them and all their consequences.

You're not deprived. You're *powerful* and use your power to look after yourself.

Feedback Loops

When it comes to maintaining your ideal weight and staying great, one final idea you might like is that of *feedback loops.*

Addictions involve negative feedback loops. Before I discovered how to lose weight, I was unhappy about how I looked, how I felt and how I seemed unable to break free from my addiction. Because I was unhappy, my Fixer tried to cheer me up using lots of sugary, starchy foods. This lifted my mood for one day but meant I gained weight, which I wasn't happy about. This was clearly a negative feedback loop.

When I was on my weight loss journey, the more weight I lost the easier it was to jog faster and for longer distances. This meant I enjoyed my jogging more and got a greater sense of fulfilment from it. These good feelings encouraged me to carry on eating well, avoiding sugar and other Fat Gain foods, so I lost more weight, which in turn enabled me to get better at jogging. This is an example of a positive feedback loop.

Beware negative feedback loops. They do not, and cannot, lead to anywhere good.

Build positive feedback loops into your life. They are a great way to make sure you continue to live your life with freedom, choice and control.

Progress Check

In this section, Step 5: 'Staying Great', we looked at various aspects of maintaining your ideal weight, once you've achieved it, and staying fit.

You will find some more information in Part 2: 'More About Staying Great' and 'More About Positive Attitudes'.

You have now completed all five steps of the Rowland Reset! Well done!

There's a summary on the next page.

The Rowland Reset: Summary

Step 1 was 'The Basic Question'. I made two key points. (1) You don't have a weight problem, you have an information problem. (2) Willpower is no power. I pointed out that everything hinges on one, basic question: *how can you change what you feel you want?*

Step 2 was 'Change Your Mind'. This was about the Want Fix, and renegotiating with your Fixer so it uses new ways to keep you feeling good. It was about the difference between fake happiness that only lasts a short time and genuine contentment that lasts much longer — in fact, it can last a lifetime.

Step 3 was 'Find Your Food'. Go on your food adventure, find nutritious foods that you actually like, focusing mainly on fresh produce and green veg. Recruit the help of your FANG.

Step 4 was 'Find Your Exercise'. Indoors or out, alone or with a friend, explore options and find which type of exercise works for you. I included four principles of exercise: DDJ, JTU, FOAM and MIDIM.

Step 5 was 'Stay Great'. Having lost weight and achieved a level of fitness, how do you stay that way and not revert to your old ways? This section was about a number of points that will help, the main one being to give your Fixer as little to do as possible by avoiding negative thoughts and feelings.

That's the Rowland Reset: the easy-ish way to lose weight and get fit.

You now have all the tools you need to achieve any realistic goals in terms of your weight, size and fitness.

I've tried to keep Part One *relatively* short and to the point, rather than clutter it up with too much detail.

Part Two contains additional information and more details about various subjects. I hope you'll find it useful and interesting.

Quick Reference Page

It's not a weight problem.
It's an information problem.

Willpower is no power.

The key is knowing how to change what you want.

Fake, short-term happy or real, long-term happy?
You choose.

DDJ | JTU | FOAM | MIDIM

The right path is still the right path, whether you
walk or run.

Just because it takes time doesn't mean it's difficult.

Negativity leads back to fat.
Positivity leads forward to fit.

How To Overcome Dependency

This section is *optional*. So far, I have explained the five steps of the Rowland Reset. For most people who want to lose weight and get fit, these five steps will be all you need.

However, you may feel that your addiction to sugar (or whatever foods have driven your weight gain) is so strong that you need some extra help to overcome it. If so, this section is for you.

If you do *not* feel you have a very strong addiction to anything, you may not need this section and you can go right ahead to Part Two.

Important - Please Read!

I have no medical or therapeutic qualifications.

If you are going to make any significant changes in your life, especially regarding food and exercise, you should first go to see your doctor or physician. Discuss the changes you intend to make and take their advice.

I do not accept responsibility for any aspect of your health. You should not regard anything in this book as medical advice. The contents of this book are only offered as personal testimony, opinion and information. I do not promise or guarantee any specific results or outcome. If you take any of my advice, you do so entirely at your risk and on the basis that every individual is different so results may vary.

About Addiction And Dependency

This section is about addiction, dependency and withdrawal. If you're overweight, you are suffering from *some* sort of addiction although the details will be different in each case. In this section, I want to explain the different degrees of dependency and suggest a good way to overcome dependency if you need to.

Degrees Of Dependency

Here's a *very* simplified account of dependency.

There are receptors in your body that monitor your blood. You can think of them as being like soldiers on sentry duty. When everything's all right, they send signals to your brain saying, 'Everything's normal. You're fine.' Whenever there seems to be something wrong with your blood, such as your blood being contaminated in some way, they send different signals: 'Red alert! Something's gone wrong! You need to fix this!'

Some substances can 're-wire' these receptors so they don't work properly. I'll describe this process using nicotine as my example but the same applies to any addictive substance.

The correct amount of nicotine to have in your bloodstream is 'zero'. However, nicotine can alter your receptors so they don't work correctly any more. They start to regard a given quantity of nicotine as the normal amount to have in your blood. When the amount falls below this 'normal' level, they send a panic signal. 'Alert! Nicotine levels dropping! Fix this!' The result is that you crave a cigarette.

This is what we mean by dependency. You *depend* on the substance just to feel 'normal'. This dependency leads to a patterns of behaviour. You get the 'alert' signal and respond by getting more nicotine (or whichever substance you happen to be addicted to).

As nicotine continues to damage your receptors, the problem gets worse and your dependency increases. This is why, over time, most (though not all) smokers start to smoke more often or try a stronger brand.

To overcome an addiction to nicotine, or anything else that damages your receptors in a similar way, you have to go through the process of *withdrawal*. This means breaking the behavioural cycle of *alert* triggering *response*. When you manage to do this, your receptors will gradually repair themselves and start to work normally again.

Weight Gain And Addiction

We can divide all addictions into two groups.

Group 1: Addictions that do not involve a substance. Examples: gambling, work, internet, video games.

Group 2: Addictions that *do* involve a substance (such as sugar, alcohol, nicotine or drugs).

Group 2 addictions can be subdivided into three groups, based on what's needed to overcome them:

(a) **The Want Fix is enough**. Your dependency is so mild that the Want Fix is all you need.

(b) **Want Fix + Withdrawal**. You need the Want Fix and, in addition, a way to handle withdrawal. You can manage the withdrawal on your own without medical supervision.

(c) **Want Fix + Withdrawal Under Medical Supervision**. The dependency is so strong that the withdrawal process causes strong, toxic reactions in the body and requires medical supervision.

Most people who want to lose weight are in group 2 (a). If you feel you need a little extra help, and are in group 2 (b), this section is for you. I'm going to describe something called the PAT Process that will help you to overcome your dependency.

If you are in group 2 (c), the PAT Process won't be enough. You will need qualified medical supervision to manage the withdrawal process.

GROUP 1: No substance abuse

GROUP 2: Substance abuse
Levels of dependency:

- 2 (a) Want Fix is enough

- 2 (b) Want Fix + withdrawal process (by yourself)

- 2 (c) Want Fix + withdrawal process
                    (requiring medical supervision)

Managing Withdrawal: The PAT Process

This section is for you if:

- You have a dependency on a substance.

- You think you can probably manage the withdrawal yourself.

In other words, you are in group 2 (b) as defined on the previous page.

This section does not apply to you if you are in group 2 (c). You will need trained, medical supervision to manage the withdrawal process.

Assuming you are in group 2 (b), what's the best way to overcome your mild dependency? Here's the best, most consistently successful approach I know. It's called the PAT process, which stands for Planned Aware Transition.

(1) Plan Ahead

You can break your physical dependency in three days. I'm not saying they will be the happiest three days of your life. However, you can get through them if you go about it the right way. Three days is long enough for the damaged receptors I've talked about to stop sending false alarms. Your addiction response will 'burn out', so to speak, and you will be free from your addiction.

So, first of all, you need to find a block of three days that you can devote to overcoming your dependency. It's up to you how you schedule these three days and obviously a lot depends on your personal circumstances. For example, if you have a Monday-to-Friday job, maybe your three days could be a weekend plus either a Friday or a Monday off work.

Next, plan *where* you are going to spend these three days, which is very much a matter of personal preference.

Some people go for the 'Home Sanctuary' option, which basically means spending three days at home. It's a familiar environment, you have all your usual ways of passing the time around you and you can sleep in your own bed. This obviously won't suit you if you feel your home environment isn't very conducive to overcoming dependency.

Others prefer the 'Change Of Scenery' option. This involves going away somewhere nice that will provide a change of mood. This could be a holiday cottage, a place by the beach, staying with a friend or relative, going on a retreat or just checking into a hotel. Some people feel the change of environment helps them in emotional terms to break with past habits. New place, new feelings, new you.

If you choose the 'Change Of Scenery' option, take care. Lots of places look idyllic in the adverts but turn out to be boring or disappointing. These negative feelings won't help you to overcome your dependency. Do your best to make *sure* the location you choose will be suitable for the purpose. In addition, avoid places that have addictive triggers and associations for you.

Next, make sure you will have *many* different ways to pass the time during your three days of withdrawal. How you do this is up to you: TV, movies, video games, reading, hobbies, crafts, walks, sleep, study, fun, social time, meditation, housework, gardening... just line up as many options as possible. *You never want one second of boredom.* Prepare well, bearing in mind that, during the three days of the PAT Process, you will sometimes feel that time is passing *very* slowly.

Obviously, it's a little easier to plan three days' worth of time-filling activities if you choose the 'Home Sanctuary' option. However, even if you prefer the 'Change Of Scenery' option, you can still plan ahead and make sure you have plenty of options to stave off boredom.

(2) Three Days To Freedom

You've planned your three days and made sure you have lots of ways of passing the time.

Day 1 arrives. The rules are simple: for these three days, you can spend your time doing anything you want so long as you don't have *any* addictive substance. None at all.

The crucial part is to *anticipate* exactly what's going to happen and how you will respond.

Here's what will happen: the receptors in your body — the ones that have been damaged by whatever substance you're addicted to — will start sending panic messages to your brain. 'Emergency! Levels of [the substance you're addicted to] are getting dangerously low! You need to do something *now* to fix the problem!' These messages may be accompanied by physical signs of stress or anxiety.

When this happens, just talk to yourself the way you would talk to a friend who is very concerned for you but unfortunately mistaken. You can do this out loud or meditate and use your internal voice. Stay calm and focused. In a slow, relaxed voice, say: "No. There's nothing wrong and I don't need to do anything. The receptors that are sending this message aren't working properly. The correct amount of [the substance you're addicted to] for me to take on board right now is zero."

From time to time, your damaged receptors will try again. This is understandable. From their point of view, so to speak, they are doing their job: alerting you to a serious problem just as they would if, say, you weren't getting enough oxygen. Each time they try to send this faulty 'alert' signal to your brain, stay calm, remain aware of what's happening, talk to yourself and repeat the same message — there's nothing wrong, *faulty* receptors are sending *incorrect* messages as if there's an emergency when, in fact, there isn't.

Enjoy your complete control over this situation. The damaged receptors can shout all they like but they cannot physically move your hands. They cannot make you reach for some sugar or a cigarette or anything else. You have *total* control. They have *none*. Each time they come back with another false alarm, just calmly face them down, re–state the facts and watch their powerlessness.

As you progress through Day 1 and maybe part of Day 2, the false 'alert' messages from your damaged receptors will increase in frequency and intensity until they reach a peak. From that point on, they will gradually recede. You will experience fewer of these faulty alerts and they will become less intense. Look forward to witnessing this process.

This will not be a pleasant experience but you can get through it. The key is to anticipate exactly what's going to happen and how you're going to respond. The rest of the time, just keep yourself occupied and pass the time however you prefer.

After three days, your receptors will have stopped or very nearly stopped sending these faulty alert messages. Any alerts you do still feel will be far weaker than they used to be. The receptors in your body will slowly start to repair themselves so they give accurate signals once again. In the case of things like nicotine or drugs, they will be reset to regard 'zero' as the correct amount to have in your bloodstream. In the case of sugar, they will recognise that 'some but not too much' is the right amount.

Congratulations! You have overcome your dependency! You don't need patches or substitutes, hypnosis, willpower or anything else. Just the PAT Process. This planned, aware transition is all you need.

What you devote to this: three days.

What you get: living *the rest of your life* with freedom, choice and control instead of addiction.

(3) Additional Notes

If the PAT process leads to great physical stress or makes you feel significantly unwell, then it's not right for you. You are in Group 2 (c) (as defined at the start of this section) and trying to manage your own withdrawal isn't going to work. You will need qualified medical supervision. Check the resources available in your area and get the help you need.

You may want to go through the PAT process on your own or mostly on your own. If you live alone, this is easy. If not, you'll need to figure out the best way to achieve three days of solitude or near-solitude.

Alternatively, you may want to go through the PAT process with a partner, your family, a friend or group of friends. Maybe you want their support and encouragement! This can work but you need to follow a few guidelines. People who are going to spend time with you need to be fully supportive and promise *they will not try to interfere*. In particular, they must not start offering their own suggestions about how to overcome addiction. They need to be well informed about what you are doing and why, and to understand that you will occasionally need to concentrate, focus, meditate or talk to yourself (when you respond calmly to the false alarms).

During the three days of the PAT process, avoid social spaces such as cafes, bars, clubs and restaurants. One reason for this is that you need to stay in an environment that allows you to *control* how you pass your time. Another reason is that, for most people with an addiction, social spaces tend to have connotations of 'fun' and 'having a good time'. These aren't helpful when you're trying to overcome a dependency.

Don't go through the PAT process with someone else who is also trying to overcome the same dependency or any other. This is highly unlikely to work. If you're going to have other people around you, they should ideally be people who are not addicted to anything.

As they say on the warnings of some medication, don't plan on doing much driving or operating heavy machinery during the PAT process. During the three days, you are going to be in a rather distracted state of mind with impaired concentration. You will probably feel anxious at some times and drowsy at others. Basically, you won't be in any fit state to drive in a safe, responsible way and your judgment will be impaired. So, find other things to do.

That's it! That's the PAT Process from start to finish. This is all you need in order to break your physical dependency on whatever substance you're addicted to.

After the PAT Process, you will no longer have a *physical* addiction. However, you may still have to deal with habits of association and social conditioning.

Habits of association sound like this: "I always have a tub of ice cream when I sit down to enjoy my favourite weekly show"; "I always light up a cigarette when I get into work"; "I always have a glass of wine on Friday night after I've put the kids to bed".

In other words, you have learned to associate a recurring event with ingesting a particular substance. It's easy to break habits of association once you know about the Want Fix and the PAT process. These are the only tools you need to realise you can have the event (watch the show, get to work, enjoy Friday night) *without* the substance. Your proof is that millions of other people enjoy the same events, or go through similar routines, without reaching for any addictive substance.

Social conditioning is just another habit of association. It sounds like this, "I really want to have fun with my friends when we meet up tonight. We *always* have a few drinks! It wouldn't be the same if we didn't."; "I'm looking forward to the party so much! I'm going to allow myself to eat whatever the heck I want."

Again, it's easy to deal with this so long as you know about the Want Fix and the PAT process. The link you perceive between (a) having a good time, and (b) ingesting a particular substance is *entirely imaginary* (and promoted by a lot of advertising). You can have all the good times you want without relying on a particular substance. It's liberating to realise this and to exert your authority over how you live your life.

If you ask people who know me, I think they would say I have a good sense of fun and know how to have a good time. I am all in favour of you having a great time with your partner, family, friends and colleagues, enjoying a good social life and getting as much fun out of life as you want. However, I'm also in favour of freedom, choice and control.

Freedom, choice and control: all good consequences, no bad ones.

Addiction: all bad consequences, no good ones.

Very few things in life are a simple, clear 'black and white' choice. This happens to be one of them.

Part Two: Additional Information

In Part Two, I want to offer a lot of additional details and information that you might find useful and interesting. Enjoy whichever sections happen to interest you and ignore the rest.

I didn't put all this material earlier in the book because I wanted to keep Part One as short and simple as possible.

Important - Please Read!

I have no medical or therapeutic qualifications.

If you are going to make any significant changes in your life, especially regarding food and exercise, you should first go to see your doctor or physician. Discuss the changes you intend to make and take their advice.

I do not accept responsibility for any aspect of your health. You should not regard anything in this book as medical advice. The contents of this book are only offered as personal testimony, opinion and information. I do not promise or guarantee any specific results or outcome. If you take any of my advice, you do so entirely at your risk and on the basis that every individual is different so results may vary.

The Ideas This Book Is Based On

I want to be clear about the ideas this book is, and is not, based on. This will help to avoid misunderstandings.

This book is based on three ideas:

- Fat hurts health.

- Fitness feels fantastic.

- Addiction bad, freedom good.

Fat Hurts Health

You can be overweight without actually being ill or unwell. However, if you're overweight, it's *far more likely* that you'll eventually suffer one or more serious health problems.

Here are just a few of the conditions known to be caused by being overweight or obese: cardiovascular disease, hypertension (high blood pressure), type 2 diabetes, gallstones, reduced fertility (men) or PCOS (women), breast and other cancers, obstructive sleep apnoea, osteoarthritis in load-bearing joints and depression leading to accidents and suicide.

[*Source: 'Metabolic Regulation: A Human Perspective' by Keith N. Frayn. Second edition. Or ask any doctor.*]

As we all know, there are no *guarantees* when it comes to health. Saints can get sick and sinners can be winners. Nonetheless, it makes sense to give yourself the best possible *chance* of enjoying good health for as long as possible. This isn't about getting your weight down to a 'normal' range. Normal isn't the point. It's about being a *medically healthy* weight for your sex and height.

Fat hurts health. I've written this book to give you the best chance of staying healthy, enjoying good food and enjoying physical fitness.

Sofie Hagen's brilliant and important book 'Happy Fat' has a chapter entitled: 'But what about health? But what about you shut up?'. I agree with a lot of what Sofie says. For example, she's right when she says diets don't work. However, the fact that diets don't work doesn't mean *nothing* works. That's like trying to brush your teeth with a sock, finding it doesn't work and deciding never to brush your teeth again.

Fitness Feels Fantastic

Fitness is one of the greatest gifts you can give yourself. What's more, it's a gift that *only* you can give yourself. And it's basically free.

During my fat years, I often thought I felt good. After a splendid evening spent sprawled on a sofa, watching a movie with a feast of junk and snacks, I thought I'd had a thoroughly good time. What I now know is that being fit feels ten times better than that. Correction: it feels a *hundred* times better.

When I got fit, I discovered an entirely new level of 'feeling good'. I felt like I was glowing. Not glowing with smugness or self-satisfaction. Glowing because my body felt better and different than before. Glowing because I knew I was looking after myself properly. Glowing because every time you exercise, you flood your body with endorphins and nature's 'happy' hormones.

It took me thirty years to discover this. I hope you won't have to wait so long. There is truly, honestly, nothing that feels as good as fitness.

Addiction Bad, Freedom Good

Addiction is the opposite of freedom, choice and control.

Any addiction is bad. Serious addiction can ruin the life of both the addict and their loved ones and friends.

Freedom, choice and control are good.

There is no upside to being addicted. There is no downside to freedom.

Anyone who is overweight is suffering from some type of addiction. It may be mild or strong, chemical or behavioural, but there is always addiction involved. My aim is to help as many people as I can to escape the chains of addiction and enjoy freedom, choice and control instead.

The less addiction there is in the world, the better for us all.

Three Ideas I Despise

Here are three ideas that I despise and that have *nothing to do with this book*.

Fat Shaming

Fat Shaming is bad, stupid and wrong. I wholeheartedly despise and condemn this practice.

No one should ever be subject to abuse, insults or prejudice for *any* reason, let alone their weight or aspects of their appearance. Anyone who indulges in this shameful practice has far more problems than the person they are criticising. This should simply never happen, under any circumstances. It's a great pity that anyone ever has to endure this kind of pathetic abuse.

We should all treat one another with respect, kindness and love. This isn't trite, hippie jargon or idealist, sentimental claptrap. It's actually a practical idea that creates the best possible society for everyone. A society that runs on mutual respect works much more successfully than one that doesn't. You should never give yourself permission to denigrate another human being for any reason.

Social Conformity

No one should be made to feel bad because they don't conform to arbitrary social codes of 'normality'. If you are not hurting yourself or anyone else, you are entitled to be whoever and whatever you want to be. Everyone should understand that diversity is strength, depth and richness.

The only society worth creating is one in which everyone feels accepted and accommodated as far as possible. I'm all for individuality, difference, choice and distinction. It can be argued that there are some practical limits. You can't design a café with an *infinite* range of chair sizes to suit *all* body types. Nonetheless, we can and should at least *try* to accommodate everyone. They can't make infinite flavours of ice cream (more's the pity) but that doesn't mean we should all be forced to have vanilla.

In this book, I am not saying anyone should lose weight and get fit in order to create a society of clones. That would be very boring. I'm saying it because fat hurts health, fitness feels fantastic and freedom is better than addiction.

Oppressive Stereotyping

This is another awful idea that this book is emphatically *not* about.

Serious problems arise when people are endlessly bombarded with images of 'perfect' models and celebrities. They can all too easily start to feel inadequate by comparison. This tends to affect women more than men, and young, impressionable women most of all. Naomi Wolf's superb book 'The Beauty Myth' puts it very well:

> "The advertisers who make women's mass culture possible depend on making women feel bad enough about their faces and bodies to spend more money on worthless or pain-inducing products than they would if they felt innately beautiful."

I wholeheartedly agree with Wolf and the points she presents with such force and eloquence in her phenomenal book. In particular, I love the chapter entitled 'Religion' in which Wolf teases out the many appalling ways in which the 'church' of beauty mythology propagates itself.

Another aspect of the same problem is any form of humour that seeks to present large or overweight people as the butt of the joke, usually implying that they are lazy, greedy or unpleasant. There are many stories, shows and movies featuring fat characters that we are supposed to find inherently amusing or comical. This is puzzling, since I doubt the writers would expect us to find anything funny about a character addicted to heroin. As I can readily testify, there is nothing remotely amusing about any addiction, including the addictions that can lead to obesity. It's a *horrible* problem to have. In fact, there's nothing amusing about addiction in general.

Having already mentioned 'Happy Fat' by Sofie Hagen and 'The Beauty Myth' by Naomi Wolf, let me also mention 'Fat Is A Feminist Issue' by Susie Orbach. These books are tremendously important and I recommend them. I particularly recommend them to all the *men* reading this: read these books because you'll find them fascinating, amazing and eye-opening. They might also help you to treat women with respect and understanding.

More About The Want Fix

In Step 2, 'Change Your Mind', I explained the Want Fix technique — how to change what you feel you want. Here's some more information about it.

I didn't invent the Want Fix. It's basically just my name for a therapeutic technique called Parts Integration, which has been around for a while. It's derived from the work of American therapist Virginia Satir, a pioneer in the field of family therapy. Even though it's far from new, I get the impression that very few people have ever heard of Parts Integration. Even some professional therapists are apparently unaware of it.

Most of what I know about Parts Integration comes from my friend James Mallinson, a highly experienced hypnotherapist who runs the 'Fix My Mind' clinic. He is a truly wonderful person to talk to regarding all aspects of the mind and how it works.

James told me that Parts Integration is based on the idea that your unconscious has good intentions that are themselves unconscious unless you become aware of them. As an individual, you create parts of yourself that reside within your own internal ecosystem. In moments of emotional significance, you may create a part such as an 'addict' whose role is to make you feel better. For example, it might use sugar as a quick way to make you feel good.

Unfortunately, your *behaviour* may be completely counter to your *intention*, which can create conflict. For example, a smoker might say, "Part of me hates smoking but part of me likes it". The therapist seeks to neutralise this type of conflict. There are several ways to do this but the basic principle is to help the patient become aware of the two parts and the nature of the conflict, and to focus on the *ultimate* intention (feeling as good as possible, as often as possible).

The therapist and patient, working together, can encourage the 'addict' to give up one behaviour (that doesn't serve the ultimate intention very well) and replace it with one that's more likely to be successful. In effect, the patient manages to create a new part that integrates the parts that were previously separate and in conflict.

If ever you want to work with a trained, professional therapist, James is the one I recommend. He's very knowledgeable, experienced and approachable.

More About Meditation

In Step 2, 'Change Your Mind', I explained that the Want Fix starts with meditation. Here's a bit more information if you want it.

Meditation is very good for your physical, mental and emotional health. It's free and you can do it just about anywhere. You don't need any special equipment and there's no need to tie yourself in knots, embrace strange beliefs or make yourself uncomfortable. I'm going to briefly describe the type of meditation I use, just in case it's of interest.

1. Choose a time when there are as few distractions as possible. I like incense so I generally light some before I start but that's optional. Sit anywhere you feel comfortable — on a favourite chair, on the edge of your bed, in your garden, on the beach... wherever you like.

2. Close your eyes and relax as much as you can. Just focus on your own breathing for a while.

3. Breathe *in* slowly, completely filling your lungs, while you count from 1 to 4. You need a tactile way to count. I rest my hands on my thighs and count by very lightly tapping my forefinger on my thigh.

4. Hold your breath for a count of 7.

5. Breathe out slowly and evenly for a count of 8. Try to exhale completely, so that by the time you get to 8 you have expelled all the air from your lungs.

6. Repeat this 4-7-8 cycle a few times. You might like to see how far you can slow down this cycle, reaching the point where you feel very relaxed and mellow.

7. Having done a few 4-7-8 cycles, and achieved a deep state of relaxation, allow yourself to breathe normally without counting, though still in a very slow, even and relaxed way.

8. You can now use your meditation time in any way that you want. You can go through affirmations about your life, your goals, the person you want to be or anything else. You can work on your self-confidence, visualise the success you want to achieve or communicate with your Fixer and go over your Want Fix. Use the time as you wish.

9. When you're ready to end the session, go through a few more cycles of 4-7-8 breathing then slowly open your eyes and re-engage with the world around you.

There are many styles of meditation. If you don't like the one that I've described, explore other approaches until you find one that you do like. You can find a local teacher, read about meditation online, watch video tutorials or ask friends.

How long should you meditate for and how often? Whatever works best for you. I generally enjoy four or five sessions per week. I set the timer on my phone and generally meditate for about 15 minutes per session. I take more time if I feel like it and less time if I'm in a bit of a time crush and have discovered, rather annoyingly, that the day that has been delivered isn't long enough to fit in all the things I need to do in it, which is clearly not my fault. I also have short 'top up' sessions lasting just a few minutes whenever I feel like it.

I learned about the 4-7-8 breathing technique from a video featuring the consistently wonderful Dr. Andrew Weil, who offers plenty of excellent advice on a broad range of health subjects. You should check out his work online.

You may also like to read a delightful book by Dan Harris called '10% Happier', which celebrates the joys of meditation. It has an excellent subtitle: 'How I Tamed the Voice in My Head, Reduced Stress Without Losing My Edge and Found Self-Help That Actually Works — A True Story'. It's a delightful, easy-to-read book and, among other things, a wonderful cautionary tale for anyone who thinks drugs are either fun or a good way to cope with a high pressure job.

More About Finding Your Food

Step 3 of the Rowland Reset was 'Find Your Food'. Here are a few additional points that you may find helpful.

Give Yourself Time To Adjust

When you go on your food adventure, give everything a fair try before you decide whether you do, or do not, like it. You might find you don't like something when it's prepared one way but *do* like it if you prepare it a different way. For example, you might dislike boiled cabbage but really enjoy sauerkraut or kimchi. Some people dislike chickpeas (garbanzo beans) yet love hummus. Explore, experiment, learn, have the adventure and see what you discover!

Don't let your tastes be haunted by bad memories. Maybe you tried something when you were a child and hated it, or have bad memories of horrible school dinners. Well, that was then, this is now. Ten-year old you shouldn't dictate what you like or dislike now.

Remember that you're not just trying a few new foods. You're also making changes to your relationship with food, how you shop, how you plan, cook and prepare meals and so on. It's a lot of changes. Give yourself time to adjust to new attitudes, feelings and routines. It's a process, not a race. The point is to enjoy your food adventure, make good discoveries and enjoy food more than you ever have before.

Two Friends: Ghrelin And Leptin

In Step 3, 'Find Your Food', I talked about various aspects of the terrible Western diet, including the divorce of food from nutrition. There's one note I'd like to add about this.

Among other problems, the divorce of food from nutrition damages the hormonal system that is supposed to let you know when you're hungry. The two main hormones involved are called ghrelin and leptin. Great names, huh? In a person who has a good relationship with food, the body produces ghrelin to say, "Hey, we need some fuel down here, eat something." It produces leptin to say, "Okay, got enough fuel now, thanks, don't need anything else for a while."

If you eat a lot of junk food and refined carbs, these hormonal responses become damaged to the point where they just don't work at all. As a result, you never feel genuine hunger or ever really feel satisfied.

Here's the good news. Once you mend your relationship with food, these systems start working properly again fairly quickly. You will gain a very clear awareness of when you really need to eat — as in, obtain some nutrition — and when you are satisfied and don't need to eat anything else for a while.

Most of the clients I work with on weight loss and fitness issues tell me they could feel these hormonal responses improve, and start to work normally again, after just two or three weeks of adopting a healthy diet.

(Incidentally, if you love Scrabble and word games, remember 'ghrelin'. It's the only English word that starts with 'ghr'. You never know when this information might come in handy. You're welcome. #addedvalue)

Fasting

Quite a few people are in favour of fasting, either as part of their weight loss journey or as a way to maintain their weight once they have reached their targets.

Let me clear about one thing: trying to lose weight by *starving* yourself is a very bad, totally misguided idea that doesn't work. First of all, it's clearly not a sustainable solution and has nothing to do with building a good relationship with food. What's more, it virtually always leads to negative feelings of being denied or deprived, which will sooner or later drive you back to overeating and addiction.

There are many different approaches to fasting and you can check them out online. One popular system is 5:2 fasting: each week, you have five days when you eat your normal diet and two days of either low or zero calories. Note that I say 'low or zero'. Some people say fasting has to mean exactly zero caloric intake. Others say it just means restricting your daily caloric intake to a significantly lower amount than usual.

Whether you should try fasting, how often and to what extent is very much a matter of personal taste and preference. I have tried intermittent fasting and I *personally* didn't get on very well with it. I find I get better results, in terms of either losing or maintaining my weight, when I don't try fasting than when I do. However, I do encourage you to read about fasting, try it and see if it works for you. It's also good for developing your sense of discipline and self-control.

Let me repeat for emphasis: never try to starve yourself thin. It's a very misguided and counterproductive approach and one that often leads to eating disorders. The idea is to build a better relationship with food, not to avoid it or fear it.

Eating Without Distractions

More than a few experts suggest that if you're trying to cut down on how much you eat, you should make sure you eat without distractions. This means that when you eat, you give your full attention to your food, eating slowly (put the fork or spoon down between each bite), enjoying it and savouring every sensation of every mouthful. The general idea is that this improves your appreciation of your food, overcomes the problem of 'mindless' eating out of boredom and helps you reach the point where you feel satisfied.

This is a good way to eat anyway, whether or not you're trying to lose weight, because it aids good digestion. You might not always be able to eat this way but at least try to be more aware and mindful of your eating, savour your food and appreciate all the great fuel you're putting into your body.

If you want a fascinating experience, try a bit of mindful eating.

Mindful Eating

You might find this an eye-opening, mind-opening experience that helps you to develop a new and improved relationship with food.

Prepare about 100 grams (3.5 ounces) of some healthy and nutritious food that you like. This will look like a small portion of food, which is the whole point. When you're food is ready, sit down somewhere comfortable and quiet. It helps to have a clock or timer nearby and a glass of water.

First, look at your food. Relax and tell yourself you're about to enjoy some tasty, nutritious food. Remind yourself how lucky you are. Throughout history, millions of people either starved or never had access to good, healthy food. Even today, many people go hungry every day.

You, on the other hand, have access to all the food you want with plenty of range and choice. What's more, it's all easy to get (you don't have to grow anything or go hunting) and inexpensive. In addition, there's a small army of 'food standards' people who check things like quality, hygiene and purity everywhere from farm to factory to your local stores. You're very lucky. Feel the privilege, sense some gratitude.

Get one mouthful of food ready on your fork, spoon, chopsticks or whatever you're using (I'll say fork from now on for ease of writing). Look at it for a moment. Appreciate how good and tasty it looks. Enjoy it with your eyes. Take your time, there's no hurry.

Bring your food to your nose and let it alert your olfactory senses. Appreciate how nice it smells. Take your time.

Take the food into your mouth and put down your fork. Close your eyes and just let the food sit in your mouth for a while. Explore the taste and texture with your tongue but don't actually chew. Be aware of the way your salivary glands react and start the digestive process. Enjoy the sensation and the privilege of having a mouthful of food to savour and enjoy. There's no hurry, take it slowly.

Start to chew your food, but chew it slowly and serenely. It's not a race. Enjoy the process and every bit of taste, smell and texture you can extract from what you're eating. Savour the complex layers of taste — there may be strong flavours but also subtle, less obvious ones to enjoy. Detect all of them as you slowly chew your food, which will aid good digestion. When you're ready, swallow your food and enjoy the moment as you take some good, healthy nutrition on board that will give you energy and vitality.

Wait a little while. Enjoy a sip or two of fresh, clean water. Then, when you're ready, prepare the next mouthful of food and go through the whole process again.

You will find that you can make even this small portion of food last 15-20 minutes, which is why I suggested having a timer handy. This is enough time to trigger your leptin response (which I mentioned earlier in this section), so you'll also feel quite satisfied even though you haven't eaten a large quantity of food.

Let me repeat an important point: it's pointless and misguided to try to lose weight by starving yourself or hardly eating anything. The point is to build a good relationship with food, not to indulge in reckless experiments with self-deprivation and starvation.

However, it is a good idea to try mindful eating. It helps you to develop a greater appreciation of food and to realise that you don't need massive portions to feel satisfied. It also helps you to overcome the terrible habit of mindlessly snacking on large amounts of junk food, wolfing down one bite after another as if it's a race while you barely even notice what you're doing.

I'm not saying you should always eat every meal in this way (which might not be practical for you). Nonetheless, I suggest you try mindful eating, enjoy it and see how it changes your perception of food and how much you really need to feel satisfied. I found it to be a very educational experience and it helped me a great deal during my weight loss journey.

Stay Hydrated

Always keep yourself adequately hydrated. This means drinking clean, fresh drinking water regularly throughout the day. This is essential for good health in general, to keep your kidneys working normally and to adequately digest your food. What's more, a nice, cool, glass of water is really refreshing.

Some experts recommend drinking a specific amount of water every day. Personally, I don't like to make it seem quite so laborious. I'd suggest you just get into the habit of drinking water whenever there's a source nearby. Stay aware of how important it is to keep yourself hydrated and enjoy a glass of water whenever you get the chance. Be opportunistic about it.

Just to be clear, keeping yourself hydrated means drinking clean, fresh water. Not a fizzy drink full of sugar and caffeine, not tea or coffee, not a 'smoothie'. Just *water*.

You may think, "That's all very well, but water's boring." I understand this feeling. Why would you feel otherwise? All your life, you have been bombarded with adverts telling you to buy drinks containing large amounts of sugar, high fructose corn syrup, caffeine and other junk. What's more, you've seen thousands of images of young, attractive people swilling these drinks and apparently having a good time. Well, sorry to break the bad news, but if you drink lots of sugary junk you won't end up looking like the happy, attractive people in the commercials. You'll end up flabby and unfit, like I was for decades. I know you know this but it's worth saying all the same.

You don't need any of these fizzy, sugary drinks. As for these drinks being 'fun', take a look at the long list of health problems I mentioned in the 'Fat Hurts Health' section: cardiovascular disease, hypertension, type 2 diabetes, gallstones, breast and other cancers, osteoarthritis and depression leading to accidents and suicide. Tell me which of those sound the most fun to you.

Water is the essence of all life (which doesn't sound at all boring to me) and it's all you really need to stay hydrated. Having access to clean drinking water is an immense privilege still denied to many people around the world. Enjoy it.

There is a theory that, on many occasions, when you feel you want to eat something your body is actually asking for water but the signal gets misinterpreted as 'eat some food'. Not everyone agrees with this theory and I'm not suggesting you have to. I just mention it in case you feel it has any merit.

Sugar In Tea And Coffee

Here's a good idea: stop adding sugar or sweeteners to tea and coffee. The fact is, it will only take you *three to five cups* of tea or coffee to get used to how it tastes without sugar.

There are several good reasons to do this. It's one more way to avoid triggering a blood sugar spike that puts your body in Fat Gain mode. Also, you will start to enjoy the taste of the tea or coffee itself, rather than its taste masked and smothered by sugar.

Don't imagine that sweeteners or sugar substitutes are a 'healthier' option. In terms of weight loss, they are no better since they can still trigger your insulin response and feed your addiction to sweet-tasting foods. Trust me: it only takes three to five cups to get used to the taste, after which you'll realise you don't *want* the sugar any more.

Here's another interesting perspective. Some people choose to stop adding sugar to tea or coffee in a rather symbolic way. They see it as a simple way to demonstrate to themselves that they can change what they eat and drink. It's a big enough change to make a difference but not one that takes long to get used to.

Incidentally, I don't actually drink coffee at all. Yes, this is possible! I stopped about 15 years ago. Although it's not strictly relevant to weight loss, let me add that giving up coffee might help you to sleep better or to experience less stress. Caffeine can stay in your system for up to 24 hours, leading to a vicious circle of tiredness. You wake up feeling tired so you have coffee to perk yourself up. Throughout the day, you have more. When you go to bed you have lots of caffeine on board so you either struggle to get to sleep or don't enjoy very *good* sleep. You wake up feeling a bit tired... so you go round the circle again.

If you don't have any of these sort of issues, great. If you do, you may want to think about making some changes.

I've had quite a few conversations with people about coffee and the fact that I never touch the stuff. Almost every time, the response I get is, "Oh, I couldn't do that! I *need* my coffee in the morning or I'm useless!" People don't seem to realise that this bright, cheerful acknowledgement of *dependency on a drug* to get through the day proves the very point I'm trying to make.

I do drink tea. I prefer what's called 'white' tea, which is made without milk or sugar. This was one of the things I discovered when I went on my food adventure. I saw it in a supermarket, had no idea what it was, tried it and found that I love it!

A Note About Fruit

When you're losing weight, should you eat much fruit? This is an interesting question that doesn't have a handy soundbite answer.

First of all, if you've been brought up in certain parts of the Western World (particularly the US and the UK) you may be familiar with the notion of 'get your 5 a day'. This is a campaign suggesting you eat five portions of fruit and vegetables per day. Ignore this. It's not medical advice. It's just an advertising campaign dreamed up by (guess who?) people who want to sell fruit and vegetables.

Fruit is good for you but it also contains a lot of fructose, which is a sugar — so you might feel it's best avoided. However, the fructose is chemically bonded with the rest of the fruit so your body has to do quite a lot of work to digest it. It's a complex carb and therefore unlikely to trigger your insulin response. In addition, fruit also contains lots of other good stuff, like vitamins and minerals, that are good for your health.

To sum up, yes, enjoy fruit because it's good for you, it's delicious and it won't trigger a sugar spike. That said, when you're *first* trying to lose weight, you might want to reduce your fruit intake to cut as much sugar from your diet as possible. When your weight comes down, you can gradually reintroduce more fruit into your diet.

A Note About Alcohol

If you want to lose weight, alcohol is one of your biggest enemies (just like sugar). It's one of the fastest and most effective ways to put your body into Fat Gain mode.

The only approach that makes sense is to cut alcohol out of your life altogether, at least until you have lost all the weight you want to. You should be able to do this using the Want Fix and the PAT Process described earlier in this book. If you can't, then you have a serious alcohol addiction and will need medically qualified help with the withdrawal process.

If you *can* manage to live without alcohol until you've reached your targets, you may find as I did that it's quite an eye-opening experience. You might realise you don't really enjoy alcohol as much as you thought you did (or as much as you have been conditioned and brainwashed to think). Once you've reached your target weight, the best plan is to either forget about alcohol altogether or only enjoy it in moderation, on a few special occasions per year and with food (as opposed to drinking for the sake of drinking).

I'd like to repeat the point that I am not for or against any particular *substance*. I am against *addiction* and in favour of freedom, choice and control. Sugar and alcohol are great servants but terrible masters. If you can enjoy them in a way that doesn't cause problems for you or anyone else, that's okay.

In the 'Suggested Reading' section at the back, I've recommended two books on this subject: 'Alcohol Lied To Me' and 'The Unexpected Joy Of Being Sober'. They're both well worth a look.

If You Want To Speed Up Results

If you want to lose weight as rapidly as possible, while staying within healthy and responsible limits, here's a good tip: get into the habit of putting your body into Fat Loss mode at the start of the day and keeping it there.

Here's the general idea. When you get up, do some exercise for at least 20 minutes. Having completed your exercise, wait at least one hour before you eat anything. You can have water and tea/coffee but no solid food. This will encourage your body to go into Fat Loss mode and start using up your fat reserves. After the hour's wait, enjoy your normal breakfast. For the rest of the day, eat correctly and take care of all your nutritional needs, but keep your blood sugar level low so you remain in Fat Loss mode all day. This plan might seem like a radically different way to start your day but it won't take you long to get used to it. You can do it!

I realise this plan might not be practical for everyone. If you can't exercise for 20 minutes, at least go for a walk. Maybe you can't even do that, because you're busy getting the kids up or you have to get to your early shift at work. You'll have to adapt the details to suit your lifestyle. The point is to be busy, active and moving around so that you put your body into Fat Loss mode.

If you can get into the habit of doing this, and keeping your body in Fat Loss mode all day, you'll speed up how quickly you lose weight. However, always eat correctly, make sure you enjoy adequate nutrition and never try to starve yourself.

It's a shame that many people are conditioned since birth to start the day in a very different and unhelpful way: get out of bed, sit down at the kitchen table (in other words, remain sedentary) and eat a sugary cereal drenched in milk. The breakfast cereal adverts make this look like a deliriously joyful experience. In reality, it's just a very good way to put your body into Fat Gain mode, with predictable results.

80

The 14 Week Challenge

If you want to enjoy a great sense of achievement, you might like to try the 14 Week Challenge. The rules are simple: no sugar, no starch, no refined carbs, no alcohol, no exceptions, no whining. If you do this for 14 weeks, you will lose weight rapidly but responsibly, learn a lot about what you can do as well as impressing yourself and everyone who knows you. I did this for the final section of my weight loss journey and found it was a remarkable experience and a surprisingly enjoyable one.

Right in the middle of my 14 Week Challenge, I had to go to Las Vegas to lecture and perform at a magic convention. (I'm not a professional magician but I dabble a bit in magic and mentalism, love the magic community and sometimes get asked to do stuff at conventions.) This trip was rather difficult for me, to put it mildly. I'm lucky enough to have been to Vegas quite a few times and I've always associated it with hedonism, indulgence and fun — great shows, late nights, have a drink, have a meal, let the good times roll! This being so, it felt rather strange to go there and stick to the rules of the Challenge. Somehow, I managed it. As well as having a terrific time and seeing some great friends, I actually came back from the trip weighing less than I did at the start!

You might wonder why I stipulate 14 Weeks. There's no particular reason. You could just as easily make it a shorter or longer challenge. I was once talking to someone about weight loss and they said, "You can't really say you've beaten your sugar addiction until you've gone without it for 12 weeks." Rising to the challenge, I decided to add another couple of weeks just to prove the point and to make it more satisfying!

Why Fast Food Companies Are Not The Enemy

As you know, there are companies that sell confectionery, fast food and fizzy drinks containing lots of sugar and caffeine. I won't name names but you know the companies I'm referring to. You see their logos on every high street and in every store. Some people think that, since I want to help people to lose weight and get fit, I regard these companies as the enemy. I don't. Here's why not.

First of all, it would be gloriously pointless of me to adopt an adversarial stance. I'm nobody: not famous, not important, not a celebrity. These companies are vast, global organisations that spend millions of dollars every year on advertising. They have a much louder voice than I do and are *very* good at marketing. I couldn't compete with them even if I wanted to. While I may not be the sharpest tool in the shed, I know I can't swim up Niagara Falls.

Secondly, I'm not against any particular food or substance. I am against *addiction* and in favour of *freedom, choice and control*. I am not against people eating a cheeseburger, having some chocolate or enjoying a fizzy drink. If you are doing any of these things while *genuinely* exercising choice and control, and without any bad consequences, there's no problem. Once in a while is fine and won't adversely affect your health or fitness.

The problem is that most people who do these things are suffering from some sort of addiction and *do* suffer unhealthy consequences. Some are addicted to a particular substance (such as sugar). Others have developed a *behavioural* addiction arising from a brain-deadening amount of advertising plus broader social factors that support the idea of putting harmful junk into your body on a regular basis. Even young children can be hooked on junk, sugar and starch, which is heartbreaking.

These big companies want to make money and I understand that. However, it's possible they'd like to be successful *without exploiting the misery of addiction*. Companies consist of people and most people, in my experience, are fundamentally decent.

The companies I'm talking about could use their massive, global influence to provide information about nutrition and exercise to people who need it. They could also help addicts to overcome their addiction by providing appropriate resources. Even if they did this for the most cynical of reasons, such as the positive PR value, they could help millions of people.

I shall carry on hoping that the people who work for these companies — especially those at the top who make the big decisions — can see the difference between running a profitable business and exploiting the misery of addiction. Maybe they'll realise that lending their voice to the anti-addiction message could have *very* good PR value.

(Note: if they want to buy a million copies of this book and distribute it via their outlets around the world, I'll give them a very good deal!)

More About Finding Your Exercise

Step 4 of the Rowland Reset was 'Find Your Exercise'. Here are a few additional notes about this. I hope you find some of them interesting.

Build A Good Relationship With Your Body

When you lose weight and get fit, you build a better relationship with your body. This is a two-way street. When you take better care of your body, your body takes better care of you. It will give you strength, speed, stamina, agility and energy — not quite 'superhero' traits but still nice to have. Let me add a couple of points about this.

A New Look

Some overweight people dislike their appearance so much they avoid mirrors and don't want to be in photographs. This isn't a good attitude to have about your appearance. You're basically trying to hide from your body, which is difficult since wherever you go, it goes too.

When you go on your food and exercise journeys, take more interest in how you look. Enjoy the process whereby you slowly but surely start to look better. Spend some time in front of the mirror and enjoy the evidence of your progress. Don't get vain or narcissistic — just take quiet pride in the difference you've achieved. Develop a positive body image and love yourself instead of trying to hide from yourself. You may also want to read up on the notion of 'body neutrality'.

Get In Touch

It also helps to develop a good *tactile* relationship with your own body. Try a self-hug. Cross your arms in front of yourself and place your palms at the top of each arm. Now move your hands slowly down to the elbows and back up again. Feels nice, doesn't it?

Gently run your hands over your stomach or any part of your body where there is fat you want to get rid of. Have a word with your Fixer, saying this is what you're getting rid of. Think good things: "This part of me is bigger than I would like it to be. I've built up fat that I don't want to have. The good news is that I'm making progress and this part of me will slowly but surely become leaner and smaller. It's not a bad part of me. It's a perfectly good part of me. It's just where a lot of fat is stored but I'm getting rid of it and fixing the problem, which is great."

Jason Fung, in 'The Obesity Code', says that, "the power of human touch cannot be underestimated." What he actually means, of course, is that it cannot be *overestimated*. He also suggests treating yourself to a massage now and again, which I agree is an excellent idea with many therapeutic benefits, both physical and emotional.

Let touching be your new way of rewarding yourself. There will be times when you do something you're proud of, promoting the feeling that you deserve some sort of reward. Try a self-hug instead of reaching for a burger or a slice of cake.

Build and sustain a good relationship with your body, both visually and in tactile terms. Never disown yourself. The human body is astoundingly complex and includes countless extraordinary systems. Love yourself and love your body. Keep in touch with it, look after it and learn to appreciate it.

Personal Trainer Required?

You certainly don't *need* a personal trainer to lose weight and get fit. It's perfectly possible to lose all the weight you want, and get fit, all by yourself. This is what I did and many others have done the same.

If you *want* to hire a trainer, and feel you'd get some benefit, by all means go right ahead. For example, if you have specific goals you want to achieve, or want to get into body-building, an experienced trainer can help. Just be aware that, no matter who you hire, they can't do the work for you. Some people seem to think that just by paying for a personal trainer they will somehow magically lose weight and get fit. This is not how it works. This is not how anything works.

Another option is to find a friend who is in good shape and ask them to mentor your progress, for example by having a friendly chat now and again. In my case, I simply had a Skype session once a week with my remarkable friend Liam O'Neill, 'The Prove-It Guy', who knows everything worth knowing about health, diet, fitness, nutrition and exercise. He's a gold mine of advice and information. Liam didn't send me diet or exercise plans. I just talked to him informally each week about my progress and he offered comments and guidance as appropriate. You may find that a similar arrangement works for you.

By the way, Liam is *brilliant* to work with and incredibly knowledgeable. He's also good fun to know and very understanding about weight problems and how hard it can be to start exercising regularly. You can find him online if you'd like him to supervise your weight loss and fitness journey.

Honesty

When I was going through the process of losing weight, I found it was a good idea to talk about it. I don't mean I became a 'weight loss bore'. Quite simply, I found it was a good idea to be honest.

First of all, it was important to be honest with myself. I needed to accept that I had been addicted for many years and that now, having overcome the addiction (thanks to the Want Fix), I was living my life in a different way. I also found it was important to be honest with other people, such as my family and friends. For example, if they asked why I wasn't doing any social eating, I told them the truth.

Being honest assists your weight loss and fitness journeys. You see, the honesty isn't just, "I had this problem and I used to behave like this...". The honesty is also about realising, "I have the ability to change, using the Want Fix, and the power to lose weight and get fit." The honesty shines a light not just on the *problem* but also on the *answer*. It highlights your ability to achieve positive personal change.

Over time, I discovered there were two more benefits to being honest with people about my addiction and the solution.

The first was that I discovered I could help people just by speaking up. My work occasionally involves giving talks and presentations. Whenever I talk about my journey to weight loss and fitness, I find that people reach out to me afterwards. They thank me because what I said helped them in some way.

The second benefit, I found, was that when I was honest with other people, they were honest with me. When I started talking about my addiction and how I overcame it, a lot of people admitted to me that they either have, or used to have, a similar problem. This led to some interesting connections.

It's very hard to tell lies and not do someone some harm. It's very hard to speak out *honestly* and not do someone some *good*.

Honesty can often be the light and warmth that someone is looking for. There are people around who have a shiny, happy, perfect life. Good for them. However, there are also many walking wounded and quiet souls suffering in silence. You never know when your words, and your example, might give them some help, hope or comfort, as well as some solid, practical advice.

Be honest with yourself. Be honest with others. It makes the world a better place.

Is Exercise Addictive?

There's a strange criticism that sometimes crops up that I thought I might as well address here.

Some people say that losing weight and getting fit is all very well, but there's a risk of simply swapping one addiction for another. After all, if you start going to the gym three times a week, isn't that just another form of addiction? If you start obsessively weighing your food and making sure you are having precisely 65 grams of carbs each day, isn't this just another bad addiction?

The answer is no, it isn't. It's easy to tell the difference by looking at the consequences. Addiction is the opposite of freedom, choice and control. Addiction is always negative and only produces bad results. Freedom, choice and control are always positive and only produce good results.

If you feel the *need* to eat foods that make you fat, you are not exhibiting choice and control. You are suffering from some kind of addiction, either substance-based or behavioural. This has unhappy consequences.

If going to the gym happens to be your chosen form of exercise, each time you go you are demonstrating freedom, choice and control. It also leads to many positive results. Likewise if you're taking care to eat Fat Loss foods and not to overeat. These choices have good and happy consequences.

That said, there is such a thing as orthorexia, which you may want to read about. It's defined as excessive concern with the quality and 'purity' of the food you eat (as opposed to being obsessed with the quantity). Take care not to go down this path. Eating in a healthy way that leads to results you enjoy is a good thing. Being obsessed about it, or about anything else for that matter, is not.

More About Staying Great

For this section, let's assume that all your *medical* needs, as determined by your doctor or a qualified medical professional, are taken care of. Also, that you have used the Rowland Reset to lose weight and build up some fitness. So far, so good!

If you want a few ideas and suggestions from me about staying great and feeling as good as you can, as often as you can, here they are. My first piece of advice would be this: when it comes to health and well-being, always consider *lifestyle* before *medication*. You have probably been conditioned to think that feeling better usually involves getting a pill, a tablet, a tonic, a supplement or something else that offers a 'quick fix' solution. No effort, no change to your lifestyle — just swallow something and all will be well. There are even some (not all) family doctors who propagate this attitude, seldom if ever discussing lifestyle with their patients and instead just prescribing yet another drug.

I acknowledge there are times when you *do* need a drug or some medication. Reread the first paragraph on this page. I'm saying that if you want to enjoy the best life you can, *outside* of your immediate medical needs, changing your lifestyle is a better bet, and less expensive, than looking for pills and supplements.

My next suggestion would be to always pay attention to your MEDS: meditation, exercise, diet and sleep. Meditate a few times a week. It's deeply enjoyable and very good for your mental and emotional health. Take regular exercise, and keep to a healthy and enjoyable diet, as described earlier in this book. Understand that sleep is incredibly important for your health and and try to make sure you get enough of it. (If you are the parent of young children, I will understand if, at this point, you respond with a hollow laugh of despair.)

Find an activity that's a nice antidote to stress (other than regular exercise) and that you can turn to more or less whenever you want to. You want something that seems to light up a separate set of mental circuits and put you into a calm frame of mind. Ideally, find something active rather than just passively staring at a screen. For example, you could do some type of arts and crafts or work on something creative.

I *love* playing my guitar which, despite the fact that I'm not very good, is a very calming, soothing way to take a break from work or change my mood. Whenever I pick up my guitar and doodle for a while, it puts my mind into 'calm, restful and playful' mode. Find your own equivalent and make it your instant mind refuge that you turn to whenever you feel like it.

Explore and enjoy nature as far as possible. I don't know what you've got near you: forests and woodlands, parks and meadows, beaches and lakes or maybe hills and mountains. Whatever's available, immerse yourself in the natural world as often as you can. Apart from all the other benefits, you'll see some beautiful sights that gladden your spirit. When Nature shows off, as she is often happy to do, there's very little that can compare — and it's a free show.

Maintain good relationships in your life. Your partner, family, friends and colleagues are all important. Nourish and sustain the good relationships and distance yourself from the toxic ones. As the saying goes, 'The way to have a good friend is to be a good friend'. Human warmth and contact is incredibly healing and therapeutic. Many of life's problems can be alleviated, or at least put into perspective, by a good chat over a cup of tea or coffee. If you can't chat to someone in real life, do it online.

Hugs and cuddles are also good for your health and well-being, as is fulfilling and enjoyable sex. If you haven't read 'The Joy Of Sex' by Alex Comfort, I suggest you do so. It's a wonderful book and delightful to read. Men are very reluctant to admit they'd like a hug or a cuddle because the vocabulary doesn't sound 'masculine' enough. This is a shame and it's something that we men really need to get over.

Make sure there is laughter in your life. If you have a good sense of humour, share it. If you don't, learn to cultivate one. Humour is a wonderful way to connect with people and to smooth out some of life's rough edges. Someone once said, 'The shortest distance between two people is a smile'. Have some playfulness in your life too. Play is important. Many creative people will tell you that they get some of their best ideas just from playing, improvising and having fun.

Do some charitable work. I don't mean just giving money, although that's a good idea as well. I mean actually give your time and effort to a worthwhile cause and doing some voluntary work. Even a few hours spent helping people less fortunate than yourself will give you a much healthier perspective on life.

Explore what's meant by critical thinking. Learn what does, and does not, constitute good evidence and good reasoning. Have lots of good thinking tools in your mental toolbox and know how to avoid fallacious reasoning. Find out what people mean when they talk about 'Straw man' arguments, circular reasoning, 'correlation is not causation' and so on. Critical thinking skills, as well as helping you to save time and money, are good for your mental and emotional health. They also help you to overcome brainwashing, which helps you to enjoy freedom, choice and control.

Finally, I would encourage you to check out the work of health and diet expert Dr. Pamela Popper. She consistently and brilliantly argues the point that, when it comes to health and well-being, we should all think less about medication and more about positive lifestyle changes.

Pamela has written many popular books and has also posted numerous excellent videos online. Take a look at some of them. She covers such a broad range of subjects that I'm sure you'll be able to find several that interest you or that seem directly relevant to your own health and well-being. You may also be pleasantly surprised — she's very good at dismantling a lot of health and fitness mythology and correcting common misapprehensions.

Those are my ideas and suggestions for feeling as good as you can, as often as you can. You might also enjoy the next section which is all about positive attitudes.

More About Positive Attitudes

In Step 5, 'Stay Great', I mentioned the importance of maintaining a positive attitude as far as you can. When you experience negative thoughts and feelings, your Fixer springs into action to fix your mood. The more *often* this happens, the greater the chance of two problems.

First problem: your Fixer might make a mistake and use an old, Fat Gain, way to make you happy rather than a new, healthy way. Second problem: your Fixer might lose faith in the new methods you have asked it to use and revert to its old repertoire.

To put this in very simplified terms:

- Negative leads back to fat.

- Positive leads forward to fit.

It's therefore a good idea to avoid negative feelings as far as possible. Of course, staying positive is easier said than done. Here are some additional notes that will help.

Positive Language, Not Poison Language

In Step 5, I gave examples of using positive language when you refer to yourself, like this:

Negative: "I'm hopeless at this."

Positive: "I might not be great at this yet, but I'm learning really well and getting better all the time."

Expressing negative things about yourself, even in fun, leads to negative attitudes and behaviour. You might think it goes like this:

"I am a loser so I tend to refer to myself as a loser (because I'm just being honest about it)."

In fact, it actually works the other way round:

"Because I *hear* myself say I'm a loser, I've started to *behave* the way I'd expect a loser to behave."

When your *words* stay positive, *you* stay positive. So there's less work for your Fixer to do, so less chance of reverting to 'Fat Gain' mode.

Positive Language > Positive Expectations

You can also use positive language shapes your *expectations*. Suppose your chosen form of exercise is cycling and tomorrow you're going to try a more ambitious distance than usual. You could say this:

> "I'm going to attempt a new distance tomorrow. I expect I'll find it pretty tough. I don't know if I'll manage it, to be honest."

By describing it to yourself in these terms, you are *conditioning* yourself to find it difficult. This works better:

> "I'm going to attempt a new distance tomorrow. It's an exciting challenge and I'm keen to see how it goes. I expect I'll do pretty well if I remember to pace myself properly. Even I don't complete the entire distance, I'll be glad I tried. And DDJ!"

This creates the expectation that you're going to find your new challenge interesting and that you'll enjoy it. This, in turn, affects your attitude and your experience of trying this new route.

It's the same with almost anything you think or say about weight loss and exercise. Routinely adopting positive language will help you in many different ways. Conversely, negative language will never help anything at all. Some people refer to this as the difference between a *threat* mentality and a *challenge* mentality. Threats are scary and negative. Challenges are fun, exciting and stimulating.

ABC: Attitude > Behaviour > Consequences

Another way to think about the use of positive language is to remember 'ABC': Attitude shapes Behaviour which shapes Consequences.

This applies to any challenge: doing a bit more exercise, preparing for an exam or job interview, deciding to quit alcohol for 14 weeks, learning a new skill, improving a relationship or anything else.

If you have a positive attitude, this fosters positive behaviour: preparing properly, doing the work, taking all the best advice you can, planning your time and strategy and generally stacking the odds in your favour. This significantly increases the chances of good results and consequences.

If you have a negative attitude, the opposite is true. If you convince yourself from the start that you'll fail, you won't prepare well or devote much time to the project, which of course makes it likely you *will* fail. Every negative attitude becomes a self-fulfilling prophecy.

Self-Doubt No, Self-Great Yes

This section is about the importance of staying positive so you give your Fixer as little work to do as possible. We've just looked at the importance of positive *language*. Here's another tip: never have any self-doubt.

There are four main sources of self-doubt:

- Yourself.

- Other people.

- The outside world.

- Fear of failure.

Here are some strategies for dealing with all of these.

Self-Doubt From You

I'm sure you can remember a time when you tried to do something and didn't do it very well. Maybe you were able to just shrug it off. Then again, maybe the experience got stored away inside you as a negative message that basically says, "I'm no good."

What's the fix?

Here's the news: it's not your job to be perfect all the time. When you came into this world, you never signed anything promising to be flawless.

Don't hurt yourself or anyone else, try to fulfil your potential and help others to do the same. If you can honestly say you're living by these principles, you're golden. Nobody can ask anything more of you.

The part about fulfilling your potential is interesting. It will involve trial and error, learning from experience as you go along. Your job is to strive and learn, doing the best you can with what you've got. This is all you can do. When your efforts turn out well, celebrate! When they don't, learn the lessons that will enable you to do better next time. Everything you try leads either to success or learning — both of which are welcome aspects of your journey.

This isn't always easy. Some 'learning experiences' can be difficult to deal with. We all take some hard punches from time to time and I've had my share, believe me! All I'm suggesting is that, as far as you can, you take the positive view and avoid giving in to self-doubt.

Self-Doubt From Others

From time to time in life, you have to deal with negativity from other people: unkind words, harsh judgments and so on. It's not always easy to deal with but you must never let it lead to self-doubt.

What's the fix?

Whenever you face criticism, I have a suggestion. Ask yourself if it passes two tests:

(1) Is it informed? Does this person actually know what they are talking about?

(2) Is it constructive? Is this person offering criticism in order to help you to achieve better results?

If the criticism passes these two tests, you should welcome it because it's *really* useful. Listen well, take notes and benefit as much as you can from it.

If the criticism fails either or both of these tests, it is literally useless. You don't have to respond in an angry or defensive way. Just *peacefully* ignore it on the basis that there's nothing else you *can* do with it.

One more way to insulate yourself from useless criticism (as opposed to the informed and constructive type) is to watch Brené Brown giving her talk about 'The Man In The Arena'. You can find it online and it's absolutely superb.

Another good tip is to realise that no matter what you do, you can't please all the people, all the time. For example, I know a classically trained musician who hates the music of Mozart. Imagine that — even a creative genius like Mozart can't please everyone! Whenever someone is disparaging about your work, congratulate yourself on being in the same situation as Mozart. The same point is beautifully expressed by this quote from Abraham Lincoln, which I love:

"If I were to try to read, much less answer, all the attacks made on me, this shop might as well be closed for any other business. I do the very best I know how — the very best I can, and I mean to keep on doing so until the end. If the end brings me out all right, what is said against me won't amount to anything. If the end brings me out wrong, ten angels swearing I was right would make no difference."

Doesn't that just say it all?

Self-Doubt From The Outside World

So far, we've looked at self-doubt that can come from yourself or from other people. The world at large can also be an abundant source of self-doubt, particularly the mass media and social media.

We hear a lot these days about young, impressionable women seeing pictures of airbrushed supermodels in magazines and feeling inadequate by comparison. Page after page of advertising rams home the same message: "You aren't quite good enough the way you are — but if you buy this make-up, maybe you will be." (I referred to this earlier in the 'Oppressive Stereotyping' section.)

It's not just young, impressionable women who suffer from this kind of toxic propaganda. No matter who you are, the world gives you plenty of opportunities to feel that you're not quite good enough. The rise of social media has made things even worse, giving you more chances than ever to decide that everyone else is doing better than you are.

What's the fix?

If you're striving to do the best you can with what you've got, then you're immune from criticism. You can't ask any more of yourself and neither can anyone else. It's fine to have goals and aspirations, so long as they come from you and what you feel you want to achieve. Don't let the media and advertisers dictate what you *should* want or what shape your aspirations *ought* to take. Their interests are not your interests. You are the expert on the subject of you.

Remember that there's no need to compare yourself to anyone or anything else — either in real life or online. You can't be anyone else and no one else can be you. Social media can be fun and useful but be careful. As the popular advice goes, 'Don't compare someone else's highlights reel with your everyday life'. I've also heard this expressed as, 'Don't compare your inside to someone else's outside'.

Finally, beware the dangers of selectivity. If you're selective enough, a chess board only has white squares on it (or black ones). It's the same with your experiences in life and your self-esteem. You can choose to see *only* the things you get right and your good points or to see only the opposite. It's healthier to see the whole picture.

Be a friend to yourself and pay *more* attention to the positives than the negatives. It's good to be aware of a few aspects of your life where you could do better. At the same time, make sure you pay *even more* attention to the things you do well, the things you've got right so far and your likeable qualities.

Self-Doubt From Fear Of Failure

We've looked at three potential sources of negativity: yourself, other people and the outside world. The fourth most common source of self-doubt is the fear of failure.

The word 'fail' has lots of negative connotations. It's natural to think that if you fail then something will go wrong or you'll be mocked or criticised. These worries can lead you to feel that it's safer to do nothing than to risk failing. Of course, if you do nothing then you'll never taste success either. You may be familiar with the old saying: 'The person who never made a mistake never made anything'.

What's the fix?

Failure isn't something to worry or feel bad about. It's just one part of your growth and learning. In fact, some people say the word 'FAIL' stands for 'First Adventure In Learning'. To fail is to learn what doesn't work or isn't the right path to whatever you're trying to achieve. This puts you in a much better position to try again.

When you were just a baby, you couldn't even walk. You kept trying and trying, always stumbling and falling over. Your parents encouraged you to keep trying and praised every small sign of improvement. In the end, after lots of failures, you gradually got the hang of it. You never felt bad or self-conscious about it. Today, you're so used to walking that you take it for granted. 'Failing' is the name we give to the process of learning.

If you're interested in this subject, I highly recommend you read 'Black Box Thinking' by Matthew Syed. This fascinating and highly readable book is about why we should change our attitude towards so-called 'failure'. As Syed demonstrates with persuasive clarity, the process of 'failing' and learning what *doesn't* work is tremendously important. In many cases, it's the only way to find out what *does* work. Even if you just read the first chapter of this mind-opening book, it will transform the way you feel about failure.

You may also want to check out the work of Brené Brown, whom I've already mentioned once in this chapter. She's a wonderful speaker and writer who, among other subjects, addresses various aspects of what is often commonly referred to as failure. Check out some of her talks and articles. She came up with one of my favourite quotations: "You're imperfect, and you're wired for struggle, but you are worthy of love and belonging."

I couldn't agree more!

Two Bits Of Psychology

This section is all about staying great. The point is to have as few negative emotions as possible so you minimise the amount of work your Fixer has to do. To this end, here are a couple of notes about psychology you might find useful.

Critical People

Some people take great delight in criticising others, usually to feel better about themselves. Consider someone who says, "There are lots of idiot drivers on the roads these days." In saying this, the speaker is implying that they themselves are *not* one of the idiots and are, in fact, a *good* driver. By faulting others, they drape themselves in (implied) virtue.

If you have to deal with people like this, realise that maybe it's just what they need to do at the time. Maybe they aren't getting the credit, respect or gratification they want from anywhere else so they're trying to create it for themselves. Maybe they don't feel loved or appreciated, or they're going through a difficult time. Never worry about this kind of criticism. It's just how some people give themselves an ego cuddle. If you get to know them better, maybe you can help them to find other ways to feel good about themselves *without* feeling the need to denigrate others.

Angry People

Angry people often provoke negative feelings. When someone behaves angrily towards you, this can easily spur your Fixer into action.

Here's what you need to know: *anger is the sound of emotional frustration.* Consider a newborn baby in its cot. It is basically helpless and lacks any way to feed itself or take care of its needs. The one thing it *can* do is make a loud noise to get attention. This is how the baby gets fed, changed and comforted. As people grow older they acquire greater independence and learn more ways of satisfying their own needs.

Life presents problems and challenges and we all respond as best we know how. When people start to run out of steps, and can't think of a way to deal with their problems, they can respond in various ways. Some just give up, withdraw and become wrapped in feelings of despair. Others choose to make a loud noise, just like the baby in its cot. They are signalling that they have run out of steps, or fear they soon will, and make a loud noise (express anger) as a strategy of last resort. It worked when they were a baby and, in lieu of better options, they figure they have nothing to lose by trying it again.

When you're dealing with an angry person, try to be patient and understanding. Life can be hard and people sometimes run out of coping strategies so they make a loud noise. Maybe it's what they need at the time in order to express and thereby reduce their pain. So long as they don't hurt themselves or anyone else, you can allow for this up to a point.

Never let an angry outburst affect your perception of yourself. The other person's anger is a symptom of *their* problem, not yours. Bear in mind that anger can't last forever. Given the way people are wired up, it's just physically impossible. Anyone who tried to stay angry for a long time would just pass out.

If someone is in an angry state, don't try to communicate with them in a significant way. This won't work. A person can be angry or they can communicate successfully but they cannot do *both*. Play for time and wait for them to burn off the adrenalin and shift to a calmer frame of mind, which must happen eventually. Once they've reached this phase, *then* you can try to communicate. In some circumstances, perhaps you can help them to deal with the pain they're feeling.

Handling Emotional Crunch Points

Let's say you have followed the Rowland Reset and things are going fairly well. You have used the Want Fix, negotiated with your Fixer, found your food and found your exercise. Maybe you used the PAT process as well. You are making progress, losing weight and gradually getting fitter. Great!

There's really only one thing that can seriously disrupt your progress: an emotional crunch point. You get some bad news, a relationship goes wrong, things get hard at work, you go through a big disappointment, somebody does something hurtful... and so on.

When you face an emotional crunch point, your Fixer swings into action and tries to make you feel better. The more upset, angry or hurt you feel, the more work your Fixer has to do. At first, it will try the new strategies that you have suggested. If these don't seem to work, your Fixer will go back to its old repertoire of methods — including Fat Gain foods (or whatever else you may be addicted to).

So, how can you stay positive even when you're going through dark days? How can you prevent your Fixer feeling that it needs to resort to its old ideas? I can't provide all the answers and even if I could they would fall outside the scope of this book. What I can do is pass on a few strategies that might help.

Choose 'I Can'

You don't get to choose whether or not bad things happen in life.

You *do* get to choose how you respond to them.

Rather than focus on what you *can't* do anything about, focus on what you *can*. You have no control over what happened. You have *total control* over how you respond. The bad news, in itself, doesn't determine anything. How you respond is far more important.

Think about this scenario. A child is in a park enjoying an ice cream cone. She's careless for a moment and drops the ice cream. The child can't think of any way to undo this so she feels upset and cries. An adult wouldn't get upset because they can plan how to reach a better situation: go to the nearest vendor and buy another ice cream. The event itself isn't upsetting. Only the response ('Good thing gone, can't fix') is upsetting.

Adult problems feel very different to the ice cream example yet they work the same way. When you're going through difficult times, you can go into 'Good thing gone, can't fix' mode, getting upset and feeling sorry for yourself. Alternatively, you can think about the square you're on, the square you want to get to and how to get there. In other words, figure out how to get a new ice cream cone. It might be very challenging and difficult. Nevertheless, every step you take towards your goal will feel positive, good and fulfilling. You might like to remember this saying: 'It will be all right in the end. If it's not all right, it's not the end'.

You Are Not Your Feelings

When bad things happen, it's natural to feel sad, angry, upset and sorry for yourself. However, although you *experience* these feelings, they neither define nor limit you.

Your feelings are your awareness of your system processing emotional change and shock. You may have heard of the 'five stages of grief' as defined by Elizabeth Kubler-Ross: denial, anger, bargaining, depression and acceptance. When bad things happen, you may go through some or all of these feelings. Working through them in your own time won't be easy but neither will it last forever. You still get to choose your plan, your direction and your next few steps.

Recognising your perfectly valid feelings doesn't mean they *limit* you. A feeling is your awareness of change and a new situation. It is not a prison cell. You can still take steps to get to a better place.

Connect Not Reject

When bad things happen, it's understandable if you feel like being on your own for a while. However, solitude is bad medicine. As soon as you can, connect with someone and talk about what you're going through. Just talking and being listened to feels much better than being on your own.

There's no shame about reaching out to people for whatever help you need. You can reach out informally to your partner, family, friends and colleagues. Alternatively, you can reach out on a more formal basis to trained professionals such as a doctor, counsellor or therapist (either in real life or online).

It's easy to feel that you don't *want* to connect with anyone. Do it anyway. You will get *tremendous* therapeutic benefit just from talking about what's happened and being listened to. The person you're talking to doesn't have to offer suggestions or solutions (unless you're asking for specific, practical expertise). The important part is just that you express yourself and feel listened to. There are times when the best healing comes from *connection* rather than isolation.

The 'Treated Me Badly' Trap

A very common source of negative feelings is the notion that someone has 'treated you badly'. This is a very common refrain. "I thought we had a great relationship but he treated me badly." "I worked hard on that project with her but then she treated me badly." "I did a lot for that organisation but then they treated me badly."

This is a delusion. It can be *very* difficult to free yourself from this delusion. Letting go of it can be a tough, difficult fight. However, it's worth making the effort. You will avoid a lot of negative feelings and also avoid harbouring grudges.

Here's the reality. Everyone is striving for the same things: some happiness, contentment, fulfilment, gratification and success. Look up 'Maslow's hierarchy of needs' if you want a more detailed list. Everyone is doing the best they can, with what they have at the time, to obtain these things.

The 'what they have' part varies tremendously. Everyone has different strengths, talents, abilities and natural aptitudes. Some people get a great start in life, some don't. Some people enjoy more luck than others. Some understand why hard work, integrity, honesty, fairness, kindness and sharing matter. Other are never given that training or those values.

No one ever woke up one morning and thought, "Today, my plan is to treat [your name] badly." Whatever they did, they were just doing the best they could, with what they had at the time, to be as happy and content as they knew how to be. Maybe what they did was wrong in the moral, ethical or legal sense. If they did something that you would never do, because you have better values and principles, be glad you learned those values somewhere on your journey. They will serve you well.

Why is it important to realise all this and how does it help you to stay great? First, it's better to see reality than to labour under a delusion. If you try to figure out why someone 'treated you badly', you'll go crazy because you're trying to explain something that didn't happen. It's like trying to solve a puzzle that has no answer.

The second reason is that it stops you seeing yourself as 'the person that someone treated badly'. This casts you in the low status role of a victim. It's a toxic way to see yourself and gives rise to a lot of negative feelings. Never harm yourself in this way. Someone who behaves in what seems to be a shabby or destructive way is showing that they don't have the personal resources to do any better. This is *their* deficiency, not yours. They are the victim, not you.

Choose Your Comparisons

Here's another aspect of staying great: choose good comparisons.

In life, you can always choose your comparisons. If you compare your situation to an obviously better one, you will understandably tend to feel bad. Alternatively, if you compare it to one that would be much worse, you tend to feel good or at least okay. I suggest you choose the 'good / okay' option.

For example, you might see someone enjoy more luck or success than you even though you've worked harder and in some way deserve it more. However, you have to remember that there will be some people who feel exactly the same way about *you*. From their point of view, you've got what *they* feel they deserve to have.

Imagine someone having a good moan about some bad news they've received. It could be a work issue or about money, relationships or any one of a dozen other things. Another person might rather unhelpfully say, "Stop feeling so sorry for yourself. Some people are far worse off than you." This kind of comparison, apart from being crass, doesn't make sense. To say you can't feel bad because someone else is worse off than you is like saying you can't feel good because someone else is better off.

100

However, it does raise an interesting point. Many negative feelings arise from the fact that life can be very unfair. Next time you feel upset about life's unfairness, you might want to consider all the ways in which life's unfairness *works in your favour*. Some people in the world don't have clean water to drink. They don't think it's particularly fair. Some never get the chance to learn how to read. Again, they don't think there's anything very fair about it.

I'm not saying you can't feel sad, upset or hurt. Of course you can. However, it's worth thinking about the comparisons you choose to consider and the many ways in which life's unfairness works in your favour. This can help you to deal with bad news, process it and gradually get past it.

More About Benefits

People sometimes ask me, "What are the benefits of losing weight and getting fit?" My answer is that life gets better.

They ask, "In what way does it get better?" I say, "Think of any way in which it could get better and it gets better in that way."

In case you want a bit more detail, in this section I'm going to look at the many benefits you'll enjoy when you lose weight and achieve a degree of fitness. I mentioned some of these benefits in Part One, but here's a longer and more comprehensive list.

Avoiding Stress

The biggest benefit of all is that exercise leads to fitness and *fitness is the antidote to stress*. A lot of people talk about stress but don't really know what it means. Let's look at this in more detail so you understand the relationship between fitness and all of life's stressy stuff.

Whenever you notice something that might be dangerous, your brain sends a signal to your adrenal gland. This produces a burst of adrenalin, which stimulates your heart and lungs to work faster so you have more energy. In theory, this extra energy enables you to fight the dangerous thing or run away from it. This is known as your 'flight or fight' response. It works automatically and can save your life in a dangerous situation. There are two things to know about it:

- It's only meant to be a quick fix. One burst of adrenalin is fine. Lots of it in your bloodstream for a long time is seriously bad for you.

- This system only works if you're fit.

Being 'fit' means *you can adjust your energy levels to fit the situation*.

Imagine a scale from 1 to 20, and your normal, resting heartbeat and breathing level is about 10. If you're fit and you suddenly need more energy, your heart and lungs can start to work harder, processing more oxygen, pumping more blood around your body and getting energy to where it's needed *fast*. You might be able to go up to, say, level 16 or 17. Your body responds well to the demands placed on it.

If you're unfit, you can't do this. Your heart and lungs have only practised going up to 11 or maybe 12.

Fitness also helps you to *relax*. If you're fit and you don't need much energy at the moment, because you're just relaxing or sleeping, your heart and lungs can slow down to, say, level 3 or 4.

If you're unfit, you can't do this. Your heart and lungs don't have the same kind of range. They may only be able to slow down to about 7 or 8, so you don't get as much benefit from your rest and sleep as a fit person does.

What's this got to do with stress?

Suppose you feel worried or anxious about something: problems at work, money worries, relationship difficulties or whatever. Your brain responds to these things just as it would to a sign of physical danger. It triggers the adrenal gland, you get a shot of adrenalin and your heart and lungs try to speed up.

If you're fit, your heart and lungs can respond appropriately, working harder to deliver more energy. If you're not fit, your heart and lungs can't do this (or not much) so nothing much changes. Since the thing you're worried about is still there, your brain tries another shot of adrenalin. This also doesn't work, so it tries another.

As I've said, having lots of adrenalin in your system isn't good. It's like constantly trying to get a machine to go faster than it can. Eventually, something's got to give. This is what stress is: the persistent experience of trying to respond to an anxious situation and not being able to.

It gets worse. When you're stressed, your body also produces a hormone called cortisol. Among other things, this leads to increased insulin resistance, which we looked at earlier in Step 3: 'Find Your Food'.

Stress is seriously bad stuff. There's no way to sugar coat this for you. It's linked to many forms of cancer and heart disease as well as asthma, breathing difficulties, gastrointestinal conditions, insomnia, depression, Alzheimer's and accelerated ageing. There are no positives associated with stress. None.

When you *exercise* and get fit, this combats stress in two ways. First, your heart and lungs can respond to bursts of adrenalin, working harder and burning off the extra energy your body is making available. Secondly, you get better at *relaxing* and not worrying so much. Fitness means less stress, which means less work for your Fixer to do in terms of trying to keep you feeling good.

The conclusion is obvious: it's a really good idea to exercise and achieve a reasonable level of physical fitness.

(Almost Certainly) Better Health

In the earlier 'Fat Hurts Health' section, I mentioned two facts:

- Being fat is not, in itself, unhealthy. You can be overweight and healthy in the sense of not actually being ill.

- There are no guarantees when it comes to health: saints can get sick and sinners can be winners.

It's a shame that some people, armed with these two facts, conclude that it's pointless to care about diet or exercise and we may all just as well eat, drink and smoke whatever we want.

Yes, life can be unfair. Some people pursue lives of peerless purity in their sanctuary of carrot sticks, yoga and serenity, yet die prematurely of something horrible. Others commit every health 'sin' in the book and are still wrestling lions in their old age. Such are the twists and burns of this cracked casino we call life.

This unfairness is the reason why, whenever people discuss health, you often hear 'My old gran' stories like this: 'My old gran smoked 40 cigarettes every day, could drink you under the table, loved cream cakes, never exercised, worked down a coal mine for 60 years, raised 14 kids, lived to be 96 and never had a day's illness in her life.'

Stories like these, though often waved in the face of people trying to offer sensible health advice, don't tell us anything. Flukes and rare exceptions are not the path to good conclusions. The way we figure out what is, or is not, likely to promote good health is to study the data from large numbers of people over a long period of time.

Here's the reality. When you get your weight down to within a healthy range, and achieve moderate fitness, you give yourself the best chance of enjoying physical, mental and emotional health. It's that simple. Everything we know about medicine supports this conclusion. Nothing we know contradicts it.

Life may be a casino, but it still makes sense to stack the odds in your favour as much as you can. There's no upside to being overweight and unfit. There's no downside to being a medically health weight (for your age and sex) and being fit.

By the way, I'm well aware that by writing this, I'm *seriously* tempting fate. I'll probably wake up tomorrow and find I've got bubonic plague, dengue fever, housemaid's knee and spleen cancer, and my leg's dropped off. Fate loves to laugh at people dispensing advice.

You Will Feel Great

This is the easiest point to be cynical and dismissive about. It's easy for an overweight person to shrug and say, "I already feel great. What's your point?"

The truth is, when it comes to feeling good, there are very few things that can match the feeling of being fit and in good shape. Someone once said that if overweight people could experience being fit for one day, it would be the best source of motivation in the world. I can't give you that experience but I can say this: once I got my weight down and my fitness up, I felt better than I'd felt at any other point in my adult life.

During the years when I was fat and unfit, it's true that I enjoyed lots of fun and good times. Nevertheless, I often wasn't happy *internally*. As the years passed and I got fatter, I didn't like feeling slow, heavy, flabby and overweight. I was privately embarrassed about my sugar habit. Most of all, I felt really bad about my addiction and my persistent failure to overcome it. When I finally did overcome my addiction, and achieve physical fitness, it felt so good it's hard to put it into words.

When you get fit, as well as feeling better than you have for a long time, you will also find it very psychologically and emotionally satisfying. Without being smug about it, you can take quiet pride in knowing that you were overweight and unfit and now you're in good shape. You decided to make a difference and you look and feel all the better for it.

Please don't be dismissive about this. You may well have a great life. If so, I'm happy for you. Nonetheless, in terms of your *internal* state, I am confident that you'll feel even better once you lose weight and achieve even a moderate level of fitness.

More Energy And Efficiency

This is one of the more obvious benefits. When you achieve your weight and fitness targets, you'll find you have a lot more energy than you did before. This, in turn, means you can be more productive and get a lot more done.

This is one of the subjects that some people get the wrong way round. I've heard people say things like, "You go running? I could never do that. I just don't have the energy." Well, nobody does *at first*. The first time I tried jogging I managed to keep going for about ninety seconds, after which I was thoroughly exhausted! It's not that having lots of energy enables you to get or remain fit. It works the other way round: being fit means you always have all the energy you need.

Better Sleep

In the earlier section on 'Fitness And Stress', I explained why greater fitness means less stress (or maybe even none at all). Less stress is good news all the way. Most obviously, it means you significantly reduce the risk of all the many health problems associated with stress and anxiety. (Want a scary experience? Go online and search for 'health problems caused by stress'.) It also means you get more benefit from your relaxation, leisure and pleasure time.

You'll also sleep better. Although insomnia and related problems can be complicated, it's true that stress and anxiety are often contributory factors. If you have any sleep issues, you have everything to gain and nothing to lose by exercising and getting fit. This *could* solve your sleep problems completely but even if it doesn't you'll feel *some* benefit.

Greater Discipline

Friends sometimes say to me, "You must have a lot of discipline to go running several times per week." I can understand it might look this way and it would be nice to take the ego stroke. Alas, it's not true. I only go running because I *want* to, so there's no discipline involved. When I started running, I did it the easy-ish way using the principles I've shared in this book. At no point did I feel there was any great discipline involved or that I was doing anything heroic. Quite the opposite. I just went jogging several times a week and enjoyed the slow but certain progress I made without even trying.

It seems to me that comments about having a lot of discipline actually misunderstand cause and effect. I think it's more accurate to say that *because* I run regularly, I've built up a pretty good sense of discipline. The amazing and eye-opening experience of gradually increasing my fitness, and enjoying all the benefits, taught me a lot. This, in turn, has helped me to adopt a more disciplined approach in many other areas of my life.

Greater Confidence

Whatever your current level of confidence and self-esteem, you will have even more confidence once you lose weight and get fit. This can only go in one direction and there are no exceptions. Nobody loses weight, gets fit and reports that they feel *less* confident than they did before. This literally never happens. If you've ever had concerns about how confident you feel, in business or social situations, losing weight and getting fit is a very effective way to banish such problems forever.

Better Relationships

Think of all the important relationships in your life: with your partner, loved ones, family, friends, neighbours and colleagues. Addiction never *helps* any of these relationships and often harms them. Being free from addiction never harms any relationships and just about always helps them. This door only swings one way.

The benefits I've described so far, such as feeling good, being less stressed and so on, are likely to have a positive effect on all the relationships in your life. It's difficult to imagine any way in which they would not. When you feel confident, content and relaxed, you're in a fairly good position to build and sustain good relationships. In addition, you're likely to be around for longer. Your loved ones don't want to attend your funeral any sooner than necessary.

Better Leisure Time

When I was overweight, I had quite a narrow view of leisure and pleasure. I felt that all enjoyable social occasions had to involve eating rubbish and having alcohol. Did I enjoy myself? Sure. I also ended up obese and very unhappy about it.

These days, I know I can thoroughly enjoy myself without eating or drinking anything, or only eating things that are consistent with my weight and fitness choices. You will enjoy similar benefits too, freeing yourself from the notion that enjoying yourself must always involve behaviour that leads to weight gain. This is very liberating!

Better Looks

No matter who you are, the fit version looks better than the unfit version.

I'm not a good-looking, handsome sort of guy (feel free to write to me and strenuously disagree). Looks have never been my strong point. Nonetheless, I know that I look better now, as a person of healthy weight who is fairly fit, than I ever did during the thirty years when I was overweight or obese.

You may say you don't care much about your appearance. Maybe you think that in today's society we place too much emphasis on superficial looks. I agree, but let me mention two points.

One, your level of interest in your appearance, and how you come across to other people, may change once you lose weight and get fit.

Two, the fact that the fit version of you will look better isn't just about shallow, superficial judgments. When people can see that you take responsibility for your health and fitness, it tends to create a sense of respect and admiration. In addition, if they know you used to be overweight, they'll admire you all the more for having dealt with the problem and changed your life for the better.

Better Teeth

When you improve your relationship with food, and cut down on sugar and junk, you'll end up with better and healthier teeth. In the long run, it's very likely that you'll suffer less tooth decay and require fewer fillings and extractions. This is a significant benefit and contributes to the preceding point about 'Better Looks'. We can't all be handsome or beautiful, but everyone looks better with clean, healthy teeth than they do with gaping gaps and grungy gums.

Higher Testosterone Levels

Here's a note for my male readers. There is some evidence to suggest that when you exercise regularly, you will almost certainly boost your testosterone levels. You may or may not care about this. Nevertheless, I think most men, if told that their testosterone level was going to go one way or the other, would prefer 'up' to 'down'. Personally, I can't say I've noticed any difference, although these days I do eat lots of raw meat for breakfast and often wrestle grizzly bears for fun.

Some women who start exercising hear myths about testosterone and worry they will build huge muscles and end up like The Incredible Hulk. Don't worry. This can't happen, never has happened and never will.

You Will Be Better Informed

The process of discovering how to change what you want, rebuilding your relationship with food and getting fit is not only hugely satisfying but also highly educational. You will be able to see past all the bad information and mythology and end up well informed about your mind, body and health. This, in turn, makes it easier for you to carry on making good choices.

It also puts you in a position to help other people with *their* journey to weight loss and fitness the easy-ish way. You will be able to help them see past all the bad information and mythology and give good advice that really helps them. You will find this very gratifying.

More Money, Less Waste

In this book, I've suggested you shift your diet towards whole foods and fresh produce, especially green, leafy veg. This would be a good idea even if the only benefits had to do with losing weight, better nutrition and (probably) better health. However, there are at least two other significant benefits.

One is that you'll save money. Fresh produce costs a *lot* less than heavily processed, packaged food that has been through several stages in a factory. The other is that you'll have a lot less packaging to throw away or recycle. Most convenience food involves an atrocious amount of packaging, leaving you to dispose of a small mountain of plastic, foil and cardboard. This isn't much fun to deal with and obviously isn't good for the environment. Whole foods and fresh produce involve far simpler packaging, and less of it, so you're left with a lot less to dispose of.

The One Downside

Having listed the many benefits of losing weight and getting fit, it's only fair to also mention the downside. I do this in the interests of balance and of giving you the whole picture.

Here it is. Here's the one disadvantage of losing weight and getting fit: you will need to become quite good at graciously accepting compliments.

You'll be receiving a lot of them!

More About The Information Problem

Several times in this book, I've mentioned that people who want to lose weight don't actually have a weight problem — they have an *information* problem. In this section, I want to provide a few more details about this. This is a lengthy section, but I believe the length is justified. Bad information is a *major* reason why so many people are overweight and obese.

(1) The Myth Of Effortless Achievement

When it comes to weight loss, a major part of the information problem is the myth of effortless achievement. This is the idea that you can achieve a significant, positive change in your life without making any effort. This is nonsense. It's like saying you want to get to the destination but you don't want to go on the journey. I also call this the myth of changeless change: the idea that you want your life to change but you don't want to make any significant changes.

The amount of effort doesn't have to be great. In this book, I've consistently described the Rowland Reset as "easy-ish". What I mean by this is that there's *some* effort involved but never enough to trigger the desire to give up. It can never reach this point because *you* make all the key decisions, such as the type of exercise you do, when and how often. You never have to make any effort that doesn't seem reasonable and within your range.

If you want to achieve anything in life, there is always at least *some* effort involved. However, there is always a market for products and services promising otherwise. The nonsensical fairy tale of effortless achievement is always with us because 'no effort' is always an easier sales pitch than 'a bit of effort'.

For example, there are companies that sell drinks, foods, pills, creams, potions and devices that they promise will enable you to lose weight without any effort. The only problem is that these products can't work, don't work, never have worked and never will. Apart from that, I'm sure they're great.

There are also companies that sell what they describe as 'slimming products', 'meal replacement milk shakes' and so on. It's easy to understand the enduring appeal of these products. Wouldn't it be great if you could lose weight just by swigging a few milkshakes? If these companies are honest, they point out — in very small print — that their products can only assist weight loss *as part of a calorie-controlled diet*.

110

You could make the same claim about literally any edible substance on the planet. You could sell chocolate caramel muffins dipped in treacle and say they 'can assist weight loss only as part of a calorie-controlled diet'. Technically, you would be telling the truth. Alas, everyone forgets the small print and just remembers the slim professional model, immaculately lit, grinning ecstatically at the camera as she chugs back another tasty milkshake.

These products don't address the causes of obesity so they can't provide a sustainable solution. In addition, they simply aren't necessary. As I explained in Step 3: 'Find Your Food', you can lose all the weight you want just by eating food from normal high street stores and markets. Also, fresh veg is significantly less expensive. Whatever else may be said about them, slimming products are certainly good for trimming your disposable income.

Another facet of the same mythology is the popularity of many vitamin and mineral supplements. Feeling lethargic and want to have a bit more energy? Good news! Just rub this little brown bottle of mineral supplements and the health genie will appear, ready to grant your wishes! The adverts don't put it quite like that but they may as well do. I think you'll find the supplements make little or no difference to anything (apart from what can be attributed to the placebo effect). A far better idea is to eat well and take up regular exercise. You'll have all the energy you want.

Incidentally, this may be a good time to mention that 'nutritionist' is not a legally protected term — at least not here in the UK, where I live. Anyone can call themselves a nutritionist. You could put a sign on your wall tomorrow declaring yourself to be a nutritionist and, in legal terms, you'd be fine. 'Dietician', on the other hand, is a protected term and anyone using that title has to be registered with the Health & Care Professions Council.

The myth of effortless achievement needs to die but never will. It's one of those zombie beliefs that roam the earth, immune to the corrective power of evidence and reasoning, forever destined to be part of the conversational landscape where weight loss is concerned. This is a major part of the information problem so please don't have anything to do with it. Losing weight and getting fit involves a comfortable, reasonable amount of effort. If anyone tells you different, they're selling voodoo and wishful thinking. They certainly aren't telling you anything helpful.

Please note that what I have said about effort is entirely distinct from the 'No pain, no gain' school of egocentric posturing. This is a very misleading and unhelpful attitude that I wish would go away. There's a note about it later in this section.

(2) The Chaos Of Contradictions

Another aspect of the information problem is that health and fitness experts contradict one another all the time. There's a section on the website (www.theaddictionfixer.com) where I give examples.

The problem is the truly *massive* amount of research data available. The National Center for Biotechnology Information (NCBI) maintains the PubMed database that anyone can consult. It currently comprises over *29 million* different articles. I typed 'osteoporosis' in the search box and there were apparently 5,226 potentially relevant items.

With this much data, you can 'cherry pick' enough bits of research to support almost any opinion. If you want to suggest that eating a ton of sugar *every* day is a good idea, you can probably find bits of weird, anomalous research that suggest you may be on to something.

Even if a researcher is sincerely trying to get at the truth, there is such a thing as personal bias. It's not hard to find reasons to reject a piece of research you don't like. You can say it is out of date, was a flawed study or only applies to one particular part of the world. There is always a way for Expert A to say that Expert B is wrong.

Another twist in the tale is that a lot of diet and exercise issues simply don't have nice, neat answers. In many cases, the data is unhelpfully inconclusive so there are no clear conclusions.

Glurp Or Plang?

I'd like to present my version of what the 'diet advice' industry sounds like, based on all the reading I've done over the years. I call it 'Glurp or Plang?'. This is a surreal parody but it's not far from the truth.

First, you read an article proving that Glurp is really good for you and gives you eternal youth. Then you see another article arguing that Glurp is basically poison and causes cancer in trees and hairdryers.

Then Smiling Authority Figure Helen pops up to say that the second article was deeply flawed, only very few hairdryers were involved and in any case human beings don't have adaptive enzyme K-folic-madeupnase which renders the results meaningless for our diet.

Next, 'voice of reason' Charles writes a book saying Helen is on the payroll of Big Evil Killer Company, who experiment on kittens. He also says her so-called 'research' ignores the fact that Glurp contains Omega Neptune 19 trans fatty fatness atoms, which are the worst kind of fatness atoms and cause heartattack-itis in penguins, van drivers and most Capricorns. He has a graph to prove he's right.

Ah, but Young Counter Culture Hero Angie, a prominent V-logger on Instasnap, points out that this absurd worry about Omega Neptune 19 is based on flawed research from 1876 that was only demonstrated to be true in caterpillars in some parts of southern Italy.

Next in line is Wise, Old, Popular TV Doctor Alan. He says Glurp is very bad for you and in any case there's no need to eat it because Plang is tastier and better for your right ankle and most earlobes. He has been on a Plang diet for 92 years and runs a marathon every Tuesday.

Then activist Trudy Popular writes in her blog that Plang is A Very Bad Thing to eat on ethical grounds, being the single biggest cause of topsoil erosion in Russia. It also causes infertility and housemaid's knee in whales.

There seems to be nothing more to say but here comes celebrity doctor, Tom Seriousface. He has a quote from a celebrity on the cover of his book so he must be right (because that's how science works). He says Glurp and Plang are irrelevant and if we adopt the Cream Cake And Sawdust diet we'll look like Greek statues and never die of anything.

Note to all 'food and diet' writers out there: **this is what you sound like to normal people. Stop it.** Your endless internal squabbles aren't helping anyone.

How Is This Book Any Different?

As we've seen, theories about obesity come and go all the time and experts constantly disagree. Over decades and generations, one wrong theory merges into the next in a seamless tapestry of well-meaning wrongness and hopeless 'badvice'. You may well ask whether this book is any different. How can you be sure that, twenty years from now, people won't look back on this book the way we look back on 19th century dentistry?

Although I can't predict the future, I'm confident this book will stand the test of time. Why? Because given all we know at the moment, there's very *little* doubt and very *strong* consensus that the ideas in these pages are practical, non-controversial and based on sound research. More importantly, *you can check for yourself* that the Rowland Reset works in the short-term *and* in the long-term. I'm not asking you to have faith in a theory. I'm inviting you to see for yourself that my approach is a practical way to lose weight, get fit and be free from addiction.

(3) Treating Journalism As Expertise

Another significant part of the information problem is people who treat journalism as expertise. It isn't *meant* to be expertise and all hard-working, professional journalists would be the first to admit this.

Make no mistake: journalism is very skilled work. The art of the journalist is to take a rather random assortment of facts and figures and weave them into a story that's easy to follow — a story that sustains your interest and reaches a neat, satisfying conclusion. Journalists have to do this incredibly quickly, against a deadline and under very difficult conditions. It's a tough, stressful gig. They are to be applauded for the great job they do keeping the rest of us informed and entertained.

Skilled as they are, journalists necessarily deal with subjects in a relatively simplified way. They have to cater to their audience and most people flicking through a magazine, or watching a TV show, don't want a detailed biochemistry lecture.

It's therefore a shame that many people, who want to lose weight, think they can get the information they need from a few magazine articles or some clips on TV or the internet. This doesn't work. To lose weight and get fit you need the big picture — a complete solution (which I've tried to provide in this book). Journalism can't give you this and isn't meant to. Every professional journalist will back me up on this.

(4) Friends With Good Intentions

Here's a part of the information problem I'm sure everyone's familiar with. If your friends and loved ones know you are trying to lose weight, they may well try now and again to offer bits of advice. Unfortunately, while they may be full of the very kindest intentions, most of their suggestions won't be very helpful and some will be highly misleading. Friends who offer words of wisdom are usually just recycling something they read or watched recently, which brings us back to the journalism problem I've already mentioned.

A common example of well-intentioned but misguided advice is the computer analogy. If you're trying to overcome a bad habit — whether it's overeating or anything else — you're likely to meet people who say things like this:

> "You know, your mind is sort of like a computer. Think of the habit you're trying to change as a program that runs on the computer. What you have to do is reprogram your mind, or delete the old program and replace it with a new one."

This is wrong. I have nothing against *helpful* analogies. However, the computer analogy is *not* useful if you're trying to overcome an addiction or modify your eating habits. You can delete a computer program with the click of a mouse or a few keystrokes. It's so easy you can even do it by accident. Your brain simply doesn't work the same way. The 'hardware' is very different and we only have a very limited understanding of how it all works.

If you tell someone that getting rid of a bad habit should be as easy as deleting a computer file, and they repeatedly fail, this can create bad feelings. They may conclude they are inadequate — unable to do something you're saying *should* be as simple as clicking a mouse.

I refer to the Rowland Reset as *easy-ish*, but nowhere do I say you can change your eating habits as easily as deleting a computer program.

(5) Unhelpful Trainers And 'Experts'

For anyone trying to lose weight, another source of unhelpful or misleading information is *some* personal trainers and fitness experts.

I want to be very clear: I admire and respect responsible trainers and fitness experts. They work hard and achieve great results for their clients. They can be an excellent source of help and guidance with some specific issues. For example, if you want to build more muscle, or train for a particular event, they can help you a great deal. I know that many of them also help people with specific physiotherapy needs. However, having met quite a few trainers and fitness experts during my fat years, I know that *some* of them are not very good at helping people to lose weight. Let me explain why.

The first problem is a failure to address root causes. Some trainers and fitness experts, when overweight people ask for help, immediately start talking about diet plans and exercise. They don't talk to the client about the causes of weight gain. This is unhelpful. If you don't get to the root of the problem, you can't get to the root of the solution.

A second problem is that, as far I can tell, most trainers and fitness experts never mention, let alone address, the Basic Question I discussed in Step 1 of this book: how can you change what you feel you want? Throughout my fat years, none of the trainers or experts I met ever raised this question. This left me in the Willpower Trap I described in Step 1 of this book. It's like being caught in a maze that always leads back to the start and never gets to the exit. What's more, I've never seen the Basic Question addressed in any book about weight loss, exercise or fitness.

Here's another issue: if you were planning an interesting journey, who would you prefer to take advice from: someone who has been on that journey or someone who hasn't? Obviously, the former. If you want to lose weight and get fit, you are going on a journey — quite possibly the most fascinating journey of your life. However, most trainers and fitness experts have never been on this journey. They've been in good shape since forever. They can give you some good advice about diet and exercise. Alas, they cannot relate to the complex emotional psychology of addiction, of a disinclination to exercise or the roots of overeating. They haven't been on the journey from fat to fit. I *have* been on this journey and, in my opinion, this experience provides important insights that can't really be gained any other way.

I'm not saying you can't help with a problem that you haven't experienced. A doctor can treat an illness she's never had. I'm saying that, when it comes to the weight loss journey, it's hard for someone who hasn't been on that journey to appreciate the problems and the corresponding solutions. They might struggle to understand why you ever felt the need to get in the car late at night, drive to the one store you knew would still be open, buy a packet of biscuits (cookies), take them home and eat the lot. I, on the other hand, can understand this perfectly. For me, it's like a trip down memory lane.

There's one final issue I've noticed about *some* trainers and experts. Quite a few seem to to offer a 'one size fits all' approach to weight and fitness problems, based on whatever *they* happen to like doing. If you have sampled a few books and websites devoted to weight loss, I expect you have come across this strange tendency.

I read one book (among dozens) that suggested we should all juice everything and live almost exclusively on fruit and vegetable 'smoothies'. If that's what the author of the book wants to do, fine. He can spend gloriously happy days shoving kale, celery sticks and old socks into his trusty juicing machine. I just don't think it's what *most* people want to do. One size does not fit all and a gloopy vegetable smoothie is not everyone's idea of a great start to the day.

In this book, I've tried as far as possible to avoid making this mistake. My intention has been to offer *general principles* that you can adapt to suit yourself and the way you live your life. For the most part I've tried to take the 'you do you' approach rather than get too prescriptive. This is far more practical and productive.

Let me repeat myself for clarity: I respect and admire good, responsible trainers and fitness experts. They do a lot of good work. However, *some* of them are not very good at helping people to lose weight for the reasons I've stated.

(6) Misguided Posturing

The sixth part of the Information Problem is macho posturing and ego drivel. You don't have to look hard online to find supposedly 'motivational' messages such as 'No pain, no gain', accompanied by a dramatic photo of someone lifting weights while sweating a lot. I've no doubt this type of imagery can be very good for the ego of the person in the photo.

Unfortunately, this sort of message does more harm than good. It perpetuates the notion that if you want to lose weight, you'll have to go through a difficult ordeal, facing up to a lot of pain and strain that you, with heroic determination, must somehow force yourself to endure. This type of message puts a lot of people off even *trying* to lose weight and get fit.

I am aware that motivational imagery of the type I've described might be produced with good intentions. Unfortunately, it perpetuates the misguided idea that if you want to lose weight you're going to need a lot of self-discipline and willpower. As I hope I have made clear by now, this is the exact opposite of the truth. It cannot be said often enough: willpower is no power. It always runs out and when it does you'll go back to your old problems and old weight.

I lost 40 kilos (88 pounds) and I never felt I was enduring any hardship, doing anything heroic or using a crumb of willpower. I did it all the easy-ish way, with no pain at all. Then again, I'm not even remotely 'macho' nor have I ever had, or wanted to have, a 'tough guy' image.

(7) An Incomplete Solution Is No Solution

Here's my seventh and final point about the information problem: a lot of people offer solutions that are *incomplete*. In her brilliant book 'Food Over Medicine', Pamela Popper offers this combination lock analogy:

> "...diet is like a combination lock. If you have to dial four numbers to open a combination lock and you dial three correctly, you don't get 75% of the results. You get nothing until you get that fourth number right."

I agree. If you're trying to lose weight, you need a complete solution. Unfortunately, you can't get this from soundbites, three minute 'healthy living' segments on TV and cheery articles offering half a dozen weight loss 'handy hints'. Trying to navigate your way through this wind tunnel of fact confetti is a hopeless task. It's next to impossible to put together all the pieces you need to arrive at a complete solution.

Please Don't Add To The Problem!

All that remains for me to say is this: please don't add to the information problem! The world already has fountains and mountains of bad advice and misguided 'expertise'. It doesn't need any more.

If you ever find yourself having a chat with friends about weight loss, or about the contents of this book, please either explain everything properly (if you have time) or don't explain it at all. Why? Because for anyone trying to lose weight, glib or superficial explanations don't help and in fact only make things worse. Handy soundbites and nifty summaries are not a good path to effective weight loss. Either explain the complete solution or don't even start.

Of course, you could also do me a big favour and tell your friends to buy this book. Or buy it for them. You know I'd be *very* grateful.

A Typical Contradiction

The preceding section was about the information problem facing anyone who is overweight and doesn't want to be. This included the 'Chaos Of Contradictions' section. Here's an example of what I mean.

There's a book called 'The China Study'. Several diet experts mention it in their work because it refers to a very large, thorough body of research. It basically suggests we should cut down on animal protein. Should we pay attention to it?

One expert say yes, we definitely should:

"Well, The China Study shows that the cancer-promoting effect was limited to animal protein. We didn't see this effect when it came to plant protein, but that doesn't mean that high amounts of plant protein don't become problematic. That's why people need to consume a high-carbohydrate, low-protein, low-fat diet."

[Source: 'Food Over Medicine: The Conversation That Could Change Your Life' by Pamela A. Popper and Glen Merzer, copyright 2013, First Trade Paper edition 2014. Chapter 2 'The Program'.]

Another expert says no, we definitely shouldn't:

"In reality, The China Study is actually peppered with half-truths and misinformation. // [It] did not reveal significant associations between animal protein and cancer, heart disease or overall risk of death. None of this, of course, supports Campbell's contention that animal protein should be eliminated from the diet."

[Source: 'Escape the Diet Trap' by Dr. John Briffa, copyright 2012, Fourth Estate paperback edition, 2013. Chapter 18, 'Prime Fuel'.]

This is just one example of the contradictions that contribute to the information problem. There are many others, as you will know if you have spent much time wading through weight loss books, articles, videos, lectures, webinars, magazines and research papers. On my website, www.theaddictionfixer.com, there's a section where you can find similar examples and submit your own.

Overcoming Emotional Resistance

If you follow the suggestions in this book, I hope you'll be able to lose weight and get fit the easy-ish way. However, you might experience some *emotional* resistance to the idea of accomplishing your weight and fitness goals. How can you deal with this?

Let's look at how emotional resistance arises. Imagine you have an important job that you want to do well. You believe the best tool for the job is your hammer, which you have successfully used for years. If you were asked *not* to use the hammer anymore, you'd feel anxious about not being able to do your job as well as you normally do.

It's the same with your Fixer. It has learned a number of ways to keep you happy (such as sugar or alcohol). When you ask your Fixer to do things a different way, it can feel rather worried. You are asking it *not* to use the methods it has learned to trust. Your Fixer's concern, which is understandable, gives rise to feelings of *emotional resistance*. It's what leads people to say things like this:

"What can I say? I like my food."

"I work hard. I need more fuel than I'll get from a lettuce leaf."

"I don't get many pleasures in life. If I can't treat myself to a bit of pizza now and again, what's the point?"

"My partner loves me just the way I am. I don't need to change and I don't want to."

"No one's going to shame me into feeling bad about my body or how I look. Society's expectations are not my problem."

All these sentiments are the sound of your Fixer getting anxious. This is what gives rise to the wild exaggeration (no one is suggesting you try to live on a lettuce leaf) and 'straw man' arguments (no one is trying to shame you about anything).

Reassuring Your Fixer

The way to address emotional resistance is to communicate with your Fixer and address its concerns. Make it clear that you acknowledge all the great work it does and the excellent results it achieves, and that you are thankful. In addition, be clear that you *do* want it to carry on doing its brilliant work.

The only difference is that you're asking it to use methods that will work even *better* than the ones it has been using so far. The old methods might seem to work but they only deliver *fake* happiness for a *short* time. Better strategies help you to experience *real* happiness and contentment more or less *all* the time.

Put simply: make it clear you're not stopping your Fixer from doing its job. You're helping it to do its job *even more successfully than ever.*

When you maintain your relationship with your Fixer, be ready to address these feelings of resistance whenever they arise. If you need to repeat your explanations, do so.

'Takes Time' Doesn't Mean 'Difficult'

A common source of emotional resistance to losing weight is the fact that it takes time. Even if you take all the right steps, it will inevitably take a few weeks or months for you to achieve your target weight. Some people get a bit dismayed by this. I'd like to make two points.

First of all, enjoy the fact that you can lose weight far more quickly than you gained it. Let's say it has taken you five years to become overweight. You will be able to get yourself down to a medically healthy weight in a small fraction of that time. I lost 40 kilos (88 pounds) in seven months. It had taken me thirty years to put all that weight on.

Secondly, just because something takes *time* doesn't mean it's *difficult.* Nothing I have suggested in this book is difficult or complicated. It's all easy-ish. Using the Want Fix is easy. Going on your food adventure is easy. Finding your exercise is easy and then it's just a case of DDJ, JTU and the other principles I explained.

So what if it's going to take you a few months to achieve all your targets? How is this a problem? I once read a story about a young woman who was thinking about studying to be a doctor. She felt daunted by how long it would take. She said to her mother, "I'm not sure about this. If I study to be a doctor, I'll be 25 by the time I finish!". Her mother replied, "Well, you're going to be 25 anyway. May as well be a doctor by the time you get there!"

Let's say it will take you six months to achieve your targets. That day, six months from now, is coming anyway. You may as well be lean and fit by the time you get there!

All of which leads me neatly to a motivational technique called the mental time machine, which we'll look at next.

The Mental Time Machine

This is a simple motivational technique you might like. Many people I've shared it with have said they find it useful.

Imagine there's a special occasion coming up, one that you'd like to look your best for. Let's suppose it's only a week or two away. You might say to yourself, "Maybe I can lose a *bit* of weight in the couple of weeks I have available but I won't be able to lose *very* much. I wish I'd started six months ago — I'd be in great shape by now!"

Most people who want to lose weight have experienced this sort of feeling. Unfortunately, you can't just hop in a time machine, go back a few months and start to lose weight earlier so you're in good shape *now*. This is clearly impossible, or so you would think.

Actually, it *is* possible! You can use a *mental* time machine.

Relax, close your eyes and meditate. In your imagination, see yourself sitting in your room on today's date one year in the future. Imagine this scene as vividly as you can.

Next, imagine Future You thinking of a goal or project you wish you had started a year ago, whether it's losing weight, learning a new skill, studying a subject or something else. See and hear Future You feeling this desire to have started something a year earlier. Imagine the little pangs of regret, as Future You says, "Aw, it's a shame I didn't start a year ago. I could have really made some significant progress by now. Damn, I wish I'd started a lot sooner."

Then imagine Future You deciding to go time-travelling. Specifically, deciding to go one year back in time to start working on that goal or project a lot earlier. Watch as Future You hops into a time machine or casts a magic spell and... whoosh! Here you are! Sitting in the present, now, today. You've done it! You've successfully travelled a whole year back in time! Congratulations. You can now make the *whole year of progress* that Future You wished you had made.

This is a simple way to achieve a fresh perspective on your time and how you use it. In this example, I've mentioned travelling back a year in time. Of course, it doesn't *have* to be one year. Your mental time machine is versatile and can travel through *any* period of time you want, from a few hours to several years.

I think this is a fun idea that can help you to decide how you want to spend the next few days, weeks, months or years of your life. See if you find it useful.

Find Your Motivation

In the section on 'Find Your Exercise', I mentioned a principle called MIDIM: 'Minor differences matter'. This applies to finding a form of exercise that you like and can also apply to finding your Fat Loss foods.

You can also apply this principle to other aspects of your weight loss journey, such as how you motivate yourself. For example, some experts suggest you find pictures of fit, toned people and keep them in a scrapbook (or the modern, digital equivalent) to remind you of the sort of body you want for yourself. This doesn't work for me. I'm a writer by trade so my mind likes words and text. My visual imagination is actually very limited and I don't have the same 'mental cinema screen' that most people have (a condition called aphantasia). This is why motivational images didn't really help me.

Instead, I used the power of words. I found short motivational messages I liked and printed them out using bold, black lettering. I placed these around my kitchen and over my desk, and updated them every week.

The point is that different motivational techniques work for different people. As I said with exercise and food, go on your adventure, try different approaches and discover what works for you. All that matters is that you get the results you want.

Of course, one thing that tends to motivate people is a sense of fun and enjoyment. Nobody needs much encouragement to do things that they expect will be fun. This gives rise to an obvious question: can exercise really be fun?

Can It Really Be Fun?

During my fat years, I occasionally glanced at articles about health and fitness. There was one thing that always puzzled me. Many experts, when talking about exercise, mentioned feeling good and having fun. I assumed they must be using the word 'fun' in some strange way that I didn't understand.

In the 1970s there was a wonderful sitcom called 'Rhoda' starring the effervescently talented Valerie Harper. In one episode, some guy that Rhoda found tiresome had been pestering her for a date. One evening, he unexpectedly turned up at her apartment. Rhoda asked him, "What are you doing here?" He replied, "I just thought I'd drop by and cheer you up." With her inimitably laconic delivery, Rhoda replied: "You cannot do *both*."

In a similar way, I used to feel you could be exercising or you could be having fun — but you couldn't do *both*. In case you harbour similar doubts, let me offer some assurances. When you overcome your addiction(s) and know how to eat in a healthy, Fat Loss way, it feels *great*. When you lose weight the easy-ish way, it's *fun* and *enjoyable*. When you start to get fit, it *feels* fantastic and is also great fun.

When I go out running, I do it for one reason: I enjoy it. In fact, I love it so much you couldn't pay me to stop. (I openly invite any phenomenally wealthy people to persuade me otherwise.)

I had plenty of good times during my fat years. However, I have *never* felt better than the day I reached all my weight and fitness targets. Nothing can compare with feeling free from addiction, healthy, fit, fast, strong and relaxed. This is where the real fun lies.

I want *you* to have the joy, pleasure and fun of experiencing these feelings too. It's one of the reasons why I wrote this book.

The Amazing Journey

Imagine some of your friends were planning a trip they were all looking forward to — one full of fun, adventures and interesting places. Suppose they mentioned this trip but said that you were specifically excluded and weren't allowed to come. This would feel rather annoying and unkind, wouldn't it? It might also hurt your feelings a bit.

I don't want you to do this to *yourself*. Don't exclude yourself from going on what will probably be the greatest journey of your life.

I've been on amazing trips all over the world — Komodo Island, the Mojave Desert, the temples of Kyoto, the Batu Caves and many more. I could tell you travel and adventure stories for hours. However, I've never been on any journey that I enjoyed as much as I enjoyed freeing myself from my addiction, losing all the weight and discovering how amazing it feels to be fit. It was the most amazing, exhilarating, joyful and fascinating experience of my life — and remember, I started my journey at the age of 56. You're never too old to feel young!

You can go on this journey too. You can experience all the same joy, fun and discovery. There is no one stopping you except you. No one *can* stop you except you.

People Management

When you go on your weight loss and fitness journey, it will affect the people around you — particularly your partner or spouse (if you have one) and your family.

Once you have decided to lose weight and get fit, I suggest that you share this information with your loved ones, explaining what you're going to do and why. If they are supportive, which they will be in 99% of cases, great. They can help you by accepting that you might start eating a little differently and taking regular exercise. There may be a bit of good-natured teasing and joking at first, but don't worry. That's just part of relationships and family life.

If they are *not* supportive, it's worth asking why. When you lose weight and get fit, you'll feel better, be happier and less stressed, almost certainly enjoy better health and be more at peace with yourself. Why would anyone who cares about you, and loves you, not want you to make these changes and achieve these results?

If you have people around you who seem determined to be unhelpful, there could be all sorts of emotional reasons. It usually comes down to fear of one kind or another: that you'll change, that you'll be someone different and not the version of you they like, or that your progress will just draw attention to *their* weight or fitness problems.

This isn't really the place to go into these kinds of problems in any detail. Your relationships with your partner and your family are up to you to manage as best you can and not my area of expertise. I will, however, say something about your *friends* and your *social* life.

Social Life

When you are losing weight, there's no need whatsoever to abandon your friends or turn into a social recluse. You can and should have just as much of a social life as usual. Let the good times roll and have fun. The only difference is that you have to think about how you want to *manage* your social time.

I don't know you, your friends or what your social life is like. Nonetheless, for most people, social occasions involve doing things that aren't very helpful when it comes to weight loss and fitness: eating Fat Gain foods, drinking alcohol, being a bit indulgent and so on.

This means you basically have two options.

Your first option is to stick to your weight and fitness plan *most* of the time, but regard social occasions as 'time off' when you allow yourself to eat and drink in Fat Gain mode. It is possible to do this, and to still *eventually* lose weight and get fit, but you're making life really difficult for yourself. You will slow down your progress and could find it gets a lot harder to achieve your goals. It's a bit like trying to go somewhere by taking two steps forward, one step back, all the way.

The second way is to simply tell your friends what you are, and are not, going to do. Your life, your choices. During my weight loss journey, whenever I was due to meet friends I simply told them in advance that I wouldn't be doing much social eating or drinking.

I still went out and had fun. I just stuck to my own choices about eating and drinking. If they wanted to go to a restaurant, I went along and either ate something that was consistent with my goals or didn't eat at all. If they wanted to go drinking, I went with them but had little or no alcohol. So long as I made my choices clear *in advance*, I found it wasn't a problem for them or for me.

If you try this approach, you may find one or two friends tease you or criticise your choices. This is perfectly okay if it falls under the heading of 'good natured friendly fun'. If it gets a bit more serious than that, and if a friend will not or cannot accept your personal preferences, then they aren't really a friend at all.

Friends will support and encourage your journey to weight loss and fitness. People who won't support your journey are not your friends.

The Four Qualities Of Successful Plans

Whether you're trying to lose weight or achieve anything else, a plan is only going to work if it has four qualities. They are easy to remember using the acronym 'STEP'.

S is for **Sustainable**. A plan has to be sustainable or it's useless. By 'sustainable', I mean it's a plan you can see yourself adopting for as long as it takes to reach your goals and sustain the success. Short-term solutions are no solution. They don't work and are a waste of time.

T is for **Tailored**. The plan has to be tailored to suit you fairly precisely. If it isn't, it won't work — just as trying to wear someone else's clothes or live someone else's life won't work.

E is for **Easy**. The word 'easy' does not mean 'no effort at all'. Picking up a pencil is easy but it does involve *some* effort. In this context, 'easy' means the amount of effort involved *does not trigger a desire to give up*. This ties in with the point about sustainability. If a plan is very difficult or strenuous, you might stick with it for a short time but that's all. Sooner or later, you'll follow the natural human instinct to say "To heck with this" (or an equivalent phrase) and quit.

P is for **P**ractical. If a plan isn't practical then it's pointless. A fitness plan that involved an extremely precise and restrictive diet, plus a vigorous workout twice a day, would probably be quite effective. Unfortunately, most people — including anyone who actually has a life — would regard it as wildly impractical.

The Rowland Reset complies with these four principles.

It's certainly sustainable. I haven't suggested you do anything that you can't happily and comfortably do until you have achieved your weight and fitness targets. In fact, it doesn't involve anything you can't do for the rest of your life.

Is it also tailored to suit you? Yes it is. It's entirely based around your likes and dislikes, your tastes and preferences and your own decisions.

What about 'easy'? Well, I describe the Rowland Reset as 'easy-ish'. There's no reason why you should ever feel like quitting. It only involves eating things you *like* to eat. It only involves doing exercise you *enjoy* doing. What's more, you only have to exercise as much as you *want* to do and *can* do — remember the 'Discover, Don't Judge' part? There's no one saying you have to try harder or achieve a certain standard.

The Rowland Reset is practical too. Because *you* make all the choices, it can't be incompatible with your lifestyle or other commitments. It doesn't involve a lot of money (in fact you'll *save* money by buying less junk and processed food). It doesn't take up more time than you can spare (because *you* decide when you exercise and how often). It doesn't call for any resources you don't have, can't afford or can't get.

The world is full of ideas about how to lose weight. Most of them fail one or more of these four tests — including the utterly misguided notion of going on a diet. This isn't sustainable (you can't go on a diet forever) and it isn't tailored to suit you as an individual.

During my fat years, one of the many programs I tried involved going to the gym *six mornings per week*. I did this for about five months. In the end, I found that this just wasn't a sustainable solution for me. Most of my clients that I work with on weight loss and fitness issues say it wouldn't be a practical solution for them either.

Why It Has To Be Tailored

Just before moving on, I want to add one point about the need for any weight loss and fitness plan to be tailored to suit you.

Many books about weight loss and fitness take the 'one size fits all' approach, based on whatever the author happens to like. If the author loves eating seaweed and cycling, they say *everyone* should eat seaweed and go cycling, as if this is the One Golden Path to success.

This is madness. People have different tastes when it comes to partners, politics, pizza, music, movies, muffins and everything else. There isn't one, single way to lose weight that suits everyone. There isn't one, single way to do *anything* that suits everyone. The only thing everyone has in common is that everyone's different.

The Rowland Reset involves *general principles* that you adapt to suit yourself. You choose what's right for you because only you *know* what's right for you. Nowhere in this book have I told you what to eat. I've just encouraged you to find food that *you* like and that will *not* put your body into Fat Gain mode. Likewise, I haven't told you what sort of exercise to do. I've offered guidelines and left you to find whatever form of exercise suits you and the way you live your life.

When you make your *own* choices, you are far more likely to make *good* choices that you can stick with so you achieve all your goals and sustain your success. This is why it's so important for plans to be tailored to suit each individual.

Is This Book Unique?

I believe this is the first and only book to:

- Explain the Basic Question and why willpower is no power.

- Explain the Want Fix: how to change what you feel you want.

- Explain the causes of obesity correctly.

- Give you a practical, easy-ish way to fix your diet and get fit.

- Explain how to achieve your goals and *stay* great.

- Fit all four of the STEP requirements (sustainable, tailored, easy-ish and practical.)

I am open to correction on this as I am on everything else.

Marketing This Book

When I was working on this book, some people said I should aim it at what marketing people call a 'target demographic'. For example, they suggested I should aim it men who, like myself, are in their fifties. This would not have been hard. I could have changed the cover design so the main colours were black, dark blue and silver — the agreed international palette of manly marketing. Then, I could have slightly changed the title, stuffing it with all the man-bait words, like this: *'The Turbo-Power Rapid Action Ripped 1000 Program For MEN'*.

You will notice that I haven't done any of this. Why not? Because I have too much respect for you and for myself. I'm not interested in reducing people to 'targets' and a bunch of numbers on a spreadsheet. To be honest, I don't care about your gender, age or any other characteristics. The labels don't matter. *You* do.

If you're overweight and don't want to be, this book is for you. All I've tried to do is write the most helpful book I can — a book containing all the information that no one told me during the thirty years I was fat and didn't want to be.

All that said, I did come up with one mildly amusing title that I was tempted to use: 'From Dad Bod To Dad God'. I thought that might have been fun.

My Story

Here's the story of my life, my addiction and recovery. It's not important and I'm not saying anyone has to read it. However, I'm tucking it here at the end of the book just in case you're interested.

(1) School Daze

By the time I was eighteen, I knew three things about exercise: it was boring, humiliating and best avoided. This healthy, enlightened attitude was formed by my so-called 'education'. Let me share the joy.

I was raised in Lancashire, in the north-west of England, in the 1960s. On some days, it was wet, windy and cold. On other days, just for a change, it was wet, windy and freezing. The weather forecast was always the same: a drawing of a man soaked by horizontal rain, with an icicle on his nose, holding an umbrella blown inside out by the wind. My home town, Bolton, was at the end of a road called the A666, a number with unfortunate Biblical connotations. Insert your own 'road to hell' joke here.

In my junior school, we had one 'PE' lesson a week. Although the letters stood for 'physical education', no education was ever involved or attempted. The 'lesson' consisted of an overweight teacher standing in the school hall and barking a series of instructions: run around, touch your toes, jump up and down. It was educational only in the same sense as chewing a cactus: I learned that I didn't want to do it more often than was strictly necessary.

We also had one 'games' lesson per week. In the winter months, which was most of them, this meant getting changed into football strip and marching towards a nearby field. The 'pitch' was a churned up mess of turf frozen into stiff peaks, like a permafrost meringue. On this uneven, glassy surface, we had to play football for an hour. This might not have been such a bad prospect if you (a) loved football and (b) enjoyed a freakish genetic resistance to hypothermia.

Unfortunately, football didn't interest me in the slightest and, far from having any resistance to freezing cold weather, I felt it more keenly than most. I have a mild form of Raynaud Syndrome, a circulation defect that means my body copes badly with cold conditions. In chilly weather, my blood does a magic trick and turns to ice — at least, that's how it feels. During every 'games' lesson, while demonstrating my chameleon-like talent for turning blue, I wondered if I'd be the first kid in the school to die of boredom and shivering.

Things were just as bad at my secondary school (high school). Again, we had one PE lesson a week and one games lesson. In the winter months, 'games' consisted of the obligatory football match in Narnia. Over the summer, which lasted about two weeks, we could opt to play tennis — a sport none of us knew anything about. By the time I was eighteen, unsurprisingly, I loathed the very notion of sport or exercise. I associated those words with tedium, frozen limbs and humiliation.

Looking back, I wish my teachers had shown less talent for sneering sarcasm plus casual sadism and a little more for actual education. The sagacious guardians of my intellectual development found time to tell me about the atomic mass of lithium (6.94) and how many symphonies Haydn wrote (106). On the other hand, they never educated me about health, exercise, diet and nutrition — four subjects that were never mentioned, not even *once*, during the entirety of my school years. It struck me as a poor set of priorities. To this day, I remain convinced I could have somehow struggled through life not knowing the atomic mass of lithium. It doesn't come up all that often.

I'm not very intelligent but I was always good at passing exams, which is an important distinction. Quite early on, I got the hang of cramming facts into my short-term memory, regurgitating them in the exam hall and then forgetting them forever. This talent for factual vomiting on demand was apparently enough to get me a place at university. Pleasantly surprised by this, I trotted off to the delightful city of Sheffield to do a useless soft arts degree and jump through more intrinsically pointless educational hoops. When I got there, I discovered to my relief that there was no requirement to exercise or play football on ice. From that point onwards, I never did any exercise whatsoever.

(2) Life In A Small Prison

Throughout my childhood, my loving and responsible parents fed me and my siblings well. It's true that we had sweets and chocolate on special occasions, but for the most part I was brought up on a proper, well-balanced diet. Somehow, with impressive rapidity, I managed to get hooked on sugar all by myself.

From quite an early age, I had a taste for anything sweet. This included every type of confectionery under the sun, as well as biscuits (cookies), cakes and anything else that delivered a satisfying 'hit' of sugar. Refined starch in all its guises — bread, muffins, pastries and so on — was my dependable friend and every bakery was an Aladdin's Cave of seductive delights. I was consistently mystified by the fact that anyone bothered with the early, boring part of a meal. Clearly, the only worthwhile part was the dessert.

In the early stages, my love of sugar and starch was simply a case of "I like the taste". Later, a complex palette of emotional factors came into play. Though moderately interesting, my first job was unfulfilling and poorly paid, in much the same way as the Sahara desert is 'poorly rained on'. However, I could at least afford to buy whatever sweets and junk food I wanted. Before long, I was using food to compensate for my disappointments and to fill a few emotional holes.

My appalling diet, and the fact that I despised even the notion of exercise, had predictable consequences. Slowly but surely, I started to put on weight. At first, the effects were not too noticeable. Though I was never good-looking or athletic, I didn't look significantly overweight either. Youth is a great concealer. My descent into fatness was helped by the fact that I have always had utterly sedentary jobs. As a freelance writer, more or less all I've ever done to earn money is sit at a desk, tap a keyboard and make stuff up. Energetic, exciting, vigorous... these are just a few of the ways my work has never been described.

In my mid-20s, I began to get a little thicker round the middle. Following the conventional wisdom, which is actually a conventional *lack* of wisdom, I joined a gym. The people there gave me a piece of paper with 'diet advice' on it (all magnificently misguided, I now realise). They also introduced me to their shiny collection of clanking, metallic relics from the Spanish Inquisition known as exercise machines. For a few months, I went there twice a week. Made little progress, never enjoyed it, always resented it.

At this point, fate intervened. The series of farcical flukes and clueless stumbles that I call my career took an interesting twist or two. As a result, I got a job that involved relocating to a remote countryside location where, unfortunately, there wasn't a gym in sight. Somehow, I coped with the grief.

As the years came and went, my addiction got worse but I still didn't look too bad. My craving for sugar and refined starch intensified. I got better at fuelling my addiction and also better at hiding it. Like many addicts before me, I perfected the art of secret eating. My 30s and 40s whizzed by in a blur of jobs, all still entirely sedentary. Though I didn't look any more overweight than many middle-aged men, I grew increasingly concerned about my addiction and the physical results.

At first, I felt I'd be able to fix the problem fairly easily. For various reasons, I know quite a bit about psychology and the workings of the mind. Time after time, I tried various ways to 'reprogram' myself and also revisited the notion of going to the gym. Nothing worked. The pattern was always the same: make some progress, relapse, end up fatter than I was before.

In one sense, it didn't matter. Life was good. I started working for myself, enjoyed some truly fantastic relationships and had a great social life. My wanderlust led me to travel the world and enjoy some interesting adventures. I played with Komodo dragons, visited Easter Island, trained FBI agents and got hired by the likes of Google and Coca-Cola. It was all good apart from my secret addiction that I couldn't escape from, no matter how hard I tried.

I was trapped in a prison cell — a very *small* prison cell. It was the exact size and shape of my body.

In my 40s, I started to look significantly overweight. As I headed towards 50, I reached the point where I was clinically obese. It got harder to find any clothes I could wear. My desperation to escape the trap intensified, leading me to consult hypnotists, psychologists and therapists of many kinds. I asked for advice, tried different ideas, read books, explored one fitness regime after another. In all my research, I never came across a good explanation of obesity and the mechanisms of addiction. More crucially, no one ever explained how to change what I feel I want. This left me trying to make myself do things I didn't really want to do via willpower — which meant, of course, that I got nowhere. Each time I made a little progress, my addiction would rise up, regain control and drag me back to sinful sugar and shameful starch. Like many addicts, I was puzzled by the fact that I could try so hard yet achieve so little.

Every day, I fought my addiction. Every day, I lost.

I have seen it suggested that fat people are lazy and happy to be so — slumped on a sofa, watching TV while gorging on junk food. While there may be some people who are happy to be like this, I believe that most overweight people are trying to fix their problem. They are striving, fighting and failing, enduring cycle after cycle of frustration and failure. Why do they fail? Because nobody ever gives them the help and information they really need.

At one point, I tried a weight loss programme that involved going to the gym six mornings per week. Think about that. You can accuse me of many things but not a lack of effort. After a few months, I found this regime just wasn't a sustainable solution for me.

The problem was that, though I tried many ways to lose weight, I never dealt with my underlying addiction. I could paper over it for a while, mask it or hide from it but it was still there, lurking somewhere inside me, ready to resurface and to control my behaviour again. Every emotional crunch point triggered a relapse and sent me scurrying back to my sanctuary, my refuge of sugar and starch. Though I never hated myself, I did hate my inability to free myself from the demon within.

(3) Ending And Beginning

Everything changed shortly after I turned 56. After a period of research, I worked out the basic ideas in this book — particularly regarding willpower and the Want Fix. At last, I had what I had needed all along: a way to change what I feel I want. Willpower was no longer involved.

For the first time in my adult life, I was free from my addiction to sugar and starch. Knowing that this time I could complete the job, I took a renewed interest in losing weight and getting fit. It was clear I'd need some form of exercise. Joining a gym for the fifth or sixth time held no appeal for me so, after assessing my options, I figured I'd try jogging. Using an online map, I planned a 5 kilometre (3 mile) route: 2.5 on the way out and the same to get back.

At this point in my life, I weighed 116 kg (255 pounds). Despite my weight, when I tried jogging for the first time I raced around my neighbourhood like a spirited gazelle, demonstrating remarkable stamina and, with athletic, confident stride, covered the 5 km distance just inside twenty minutes. Of course, none of this is true.

What actually happened was slightly different. The first time I went jogging, I looked like Captain Flabtastic from Planet Wobblegut. I managed to jog, in a plodding and laborious style, for about ninety seconds, by which point I was exhausted and had to stop. Bent over with my hands on my knees, I was red-faced, out of breath and wheezing like dusty bagpipes. Applying the Discover Don't Judge principle, I didn't feel bad about this. I had discovered that I was unfit and terrible at jogging, which wasn't exactly a newsflash. Pleased to have at least made a start, I walked the rest of my route. Slowly. With rests.

After that impressive start, I went jogging three or four times a week. Slowly but surely, I made small improvements. Before long, I managed to keep going for two entire minutes, which felt like an astonishing achievement worthy of an Olympic medal. After almost exactly three months, I managed to run 5 km (3 miles). Four months later, I was up to 10 km (6 miles).

The process of gradually getting fit was a magical experience, full of strange discoveries and interesting revelations. In fact, I'd say it was the single most amazing experience of my life (and I've had a lot of amazing experiences). For example, despite my doubts, I found that jogging isn't actually boring at all. When I'm out jogging, I'm constantly adjusting my pace, trying to achieve the optimum balance between fast (because I want to see how quickly I can go) and slow (to conserve my energy and make sure I last the distance). This calls for a lot of fine tuning as I go along.

134

At the same time, I'm managing my breathing, my stride and balance, pronation (correct running action) and how my feet, legs and the rest of my body feel. I'm also keeping my eyes and ears open, taking in the scenery and noticing anything interesting.

As well as discovering that jogging isn't boring, I also learned just how good it feels! Of course, it didn't feel very enjoyable at first because I was slow, heavy and flabby. However, it didn't take long for me to start feeling really good after I'd been running. I noticed that one or two hours after a good run, I experienced a sort of 'glowing' feeling throughout my body that felt wonderful. After decades of harming my body with my sugary, sedentary lifestyle, I could tell some very significant changes were taking place. Little by little, I was getting leaner, stronger and fitter, able to complete my 5k and 10k distances with relative ease.

After my first year of jogging, I found a gym I could just about tolerate in small doses and added a small number of fairly brief visits for basic strength training. It's a strained relationship — I don't love it but I *can* put up with it.

(4) A New Life

I got my weight down from 116 kg (256 lb) to 76 kg (168 lb). Loss = 40 kg (88 lb) or 34% of my original weight.

I got my waist down from 117 cm (46 inches) to 86 cm (34 inches).

In terms of fitness, I went from zero to fairly good. These days I run about 25 km (15 miles) per week. The addiction didn't come back to reclaim me. *It couldn't come back because it wasn't there anymore.*

My decades of hopeless addiction were over. At last, I could enjoy freedom, choice and control. From my experience, I was able to devise the five steps I presented in Part One of this book.

From time to time, I do bits of public speaking. I started sharing the story of my addiction and how it had led to two types of embarrassment. The first was my embarrassment about the addiction itself. The second was my awareness that it looked like a fairly childish or juvenile problem. Some addictions, such as alcohol, smoking and drugs, though they may be terrible are at least perceived as 'adult' problems. Mine had been different, based on a craving for sugar, sweets and chocolate. I often bought the kind of confectionery that's intended for children, which is why the packaging features bright colours and cartoon characters. It felt like a 'childish' addiction, one that shouldn't affect an adult in the sixth decade of his life.

When I started talking about my story in public, a strange thing happened. Lots of other people, especially men, started getting in touch to say that they had a similar problem. They appreciated that I had chosen to talk about my addiction openly, because it made them feel less alone and isolated.

Very often, when people discuss books they focus on bestsellers that sell eleventy gazillion copies and make a lot of money. This book might barely sell at all but I don't care. Here's the way I see it. If I can help just *one* person to go from addiction to freedom, to lose weight and get fit, I will feel this book was worth writing.

I hope you go on your own journey, lose weight and get fit the easy-ish way.

It's worth it.

You're worth it.

That's my story. This is my book for you.

Let's Work Together!

Would you like me to help you with your addiction issues, or mentor you on your weight loss and fitness journey? You can hire me! I help people all the time via Skype or Zoom. For details see www.theaddictionfixer.com .

I also give talks, training and keynotes about overcoming addiction. Why not hire me to give a talk for your company or organisation, or at your next conference. What could be more worthwhile than helping everyone to live life without addiction?

I'd love to work with you. Let's build a world without addiction.

— Ian Rowland

www.theaddictionfixer.com

www.ianrowland.com

Please Will You Help Me?

If you'd like to support me and my work, please tell all your friends about this book and my various websites.

I'm self-employed, a one-man band. I try to promote my work as best I can but a little extra help is always welcome. If you can help me to 'spread the word', I would be very grateful.

For example, you can mention me to your friends in real life or on social media. Wherever people are discussing addiction, weight loss and fitness, I'd love it if you could give me and my books a mention and pass on the link:
www.theaddictionfixer.com

Got contacts in broadcast or online media? Tell them about me or about this book. They might get a good story, article or feature out of it — if you've got an audience, I've got content!

Maybe you can help me to get media appearances or to get booked to give a talk or presentation. I'd appreciate whatever help you want to offer.

I want to create a world without addiction but I can't do it on my own. I need your help to do it. Remember, it's a good idea to be kind and helpful. As the Chinese proverb says, "A bit of fragrance always clings to the hand that gives the rose."

Thank you!

Final Words

We've reached the end of this book.

You now have all the information you need. You know about the Basic Question and the Willpower Trap. You know how to change what you feel you want, fix your relationship with food, live your life for you instead of a fast food company's profits, and enjoy the fantastic feeling of fitness.

I hope you choose a new life, new ways, new you. Live the healthiest and happiest life you can live, with fitness, strength, vitality, energy and *lots* of people complimenting you on your success!

I believe in celebrating all that's best in this life. You deserve the best and you can have the best. The best, most nutritious, most satisfying food (that won't sacrifice your health). The best relationship with your body, the fantastic feeling of fitness and the end of stress. You deserve all this and you can choose it for yourself.

If you want to get in touch, my email address is ian@ianrowland.com (or just visit any of my websites and use the email link provided). I'd love to hear from you.

— Ian Rowland

London, 2020

---

www.theaddictionfixer.com
About overcoming addictions in general and weight loss/getting fit in particular.

www.ianrowland.com
About my work as a writer, speaker and trainer.

www.coldreadingsuccess.com
My website devoted to the art of cold reading.

Love And Gratitude

I want to place on record my thanks to everyone who has contributed to this book in one way or another.

Liam O'Neill, also known as 'The Prove-It Guy', was a great friend during my weight loss and fitness journey, as well as being a terrific source of inspiration, advice, information and fun. He mentored my progress week by week and made my journey a lot easier and more enjoyable than it would have been otherwise.

Julia Cotterill provided invaluable help during the writing of this book and suggested several of the sources that I consulted. She also reviewed a pre-publication draft and offered very thorough notes and constructive criticism.

James Mallinson explained 'Parts Integration' to me, from his perspective as a knowledgeable and highly experienced hypnotherapist, and provided helpful guidance.

AJ Green, who has been a good friend for many years and has worked with me on numerous projects, was very supportive during my weight loss journey and the preparation of this book.

Sal Dhalla, 'The Food Witch', helped me with several sections of this book and was always on hand to answer questions and provide feedback. She also kept me supplied with her glorious Matcha Mochi Cakes, than which there can be no greater gift.

Joan Du Kore was immensely helpful when I had to visit Las Vegas (where she lives) while trying to eat healthily and keep myself on track. She personally made sure I had a good supply of healthy, nutritious food during my stay so I didn't have to rely on junk alternatives.

Lulu Kyriacou, who always has a very positive and helpful attitude, reviewed a pre-publication draft of this book and offered very helpful notes and feedback.

Laylah Garner assisted me with the cover design. She's an excellent graphic designer who has often helped me over the years.

Barry Cooper did the proofreading and did it very well. He gets the credit for everything that's right while I take the blame for anything that's wrong.

Suggested Reading

Just because I recommend a book doesn't mean that I completely agree with the author about everything. It's possible to think a book is worth reading even if I disagree with a few points here and there. Also note that some of these authors disagree with one another.

Bach, Richard. **Illusions**. This book has nothing specifically to do with health or fitness. I'm mentioning it here because it changed my life when I was about 16 and I know it has inspired many other people as well. It's a wonderful story (about what would happen if a Messiah just wanted to give up the job) and might help you to re-think how you want to live your life.

Beck, Craig. '**Alcohol Lied To Me**'. A rightly popular and influential book that presents a very good case for giving up alcohol. Readable and persuasive.

Briffa, John. '**Escape the Diet Trap**'. Plenty of in-depth advice about why diets don't work.

Briers, Dr. Stephen. '**Brilliant Cognitive Behavioural Therapy**'. If you want an introduction to Cognitive Behavioural Therapy it's hard to imagine anything better than this. Briers has written a clear, easy to follow book that explains all the central principles of CBT in layman's language.

Carlisle, Belinda. '**Lips Unsealed**'. This is the internationally famous singer's own account of her various problems with addiction and how she overcame them. It is beautifully well written, highly readable and inspirational. Famous people are rarely this candid or eloquent about their own story. The book provides a fascinating account of what a rise to global stardom feels like from the inside. At the same time, Carlisle is bravely and brutally honest about her struggles with addiction. Highly recommended.

Duhigg, Charles. '**The Power Of Habit**'. How to take your innate tendency to form new habits and channel it in a positive direction. I personally didn't get as much out of this book as its reputation had led me to expect, but each to their own. It's a hugely popular book and I feel sure it contains much that is of value.

Frayn, Keith N. '**Metabolic Regulation: A Human Perspective**'. A detailed textbook for anyone seeking an in-depth analysis of how the human body digests food and uses energy. It's not exactly light reading nor is it meant to be, but it is admirably thorough and clear.

Friedman, Barry. '**I Love Me More Than Sugar**'. An eye-opening book about sugar based on the author's '30 Days Sugar Free' challenge which he ran online for many years. Very informative and easy to read, even if you're not interested in the many case studies of people who have completed their 30 Days challenge. Friedman has numerous interesting videos online.

Fung, Jason. '**The Obesity Code / Unlocking The Secrets Of Weight Loss**'. A very readable, enjoyable and informative book dispelling many of the myths surrounding obesity and weight loss. The first part of the book very effectively dismantles the persistent myth that eating less, or 'caloric reduction', is a good way to lose weight.

Grey, Catherine. '**The Unexpected Joy Of Being Sober**'. An excellent book about the reasons for, and benefits of, giving up alcohol.

Hagen, Sofie. '**Happy Fat**'. A very important book that is also very funny. I don't agree with everything Hagen says, but she's right about diets and many other approaches to weight loss that just don't work.

Hanh, Thich Nhat. '**The Miracle Of Mindfulness**'. I found this guide to meditation and mindfulness, written by a Zen Master, useful, fascinating and intriguing.

Harris, Dan. '**10% Happier**'. A highly enjoyable, fun-to-read account of the author's voyage into meditation and other forms of self-help.

Maclaren, Don and Morton, James. '**Biochemistry For Sport And Exercise Metabolism**'. The title says it all. Most of this very detailed textbook went way over my head, but if you want to understand some of the biochemistry of food, digestion, metabolism and fitness, this could be a good place to start.

O'Neill, Liam. '**Limitation Is A Mirage**'. A great book by a remarkable man. If you want an inspirational book addressing health, fitness, nutrition, personal development and well-being, this is the book for you. Full disclosure: I helped Liam to produce this book but all the ideas and content are his and I don't make any money from sales.

Orbach, Susie. '**Fat Is A Feminist Issue**'. The 1978 classic that has stood the test of time and is simply essential reading for anyone interested in the issues surrounding fat, sexual politics and female dieting.

Peters, Prof. Steve. '**The Chimp Paradox**'. It's described as a 'powerful mind management model'. I'm not sure about that but this book does offer a highly readable account of different areas of your brain, how they sometimes come into conflict and how you can avoid this happening.

Pollan, Michael. '**In Defense Of Food**'. A superb book by a brilliant writer. Pollan writes more sense about food, diet, health and nutrition than anyone else I know. It's hard to imagine anyone could read this book and *not* learn something useful from it. I love Pollan's memorable seven words of advice for planning your diet: "Eat food. Not too much. Mostly plants."

Popper, Pamela and Merzer, Glen. '**Food Over Medicine: The Conversation That Could Change Your Life**'. I find a lot to admire about Pamela Popper. You can find many videos online in which she brings a great deal of common sense to bear on various aspects of health, diet and medical science. I agree with her that the correct remedy for many health issues is, or should be, for the patient to change their diet and lifestyle rather than take a drug. The book is written as a conversation between Popper and Merzer and promotes Popper's Wellness Forum.

Rubin, Gretchen. '**Better Than Before**'. The wonderful Rubin, perhaps most famous for her 2009 book 'The Happiness Project', here looks at the way different personality types learn new habits and behaviours in different ways. Well worth reading and useful if you feel you need a bit of extra help adopting new habits.

Taubes, Gary. '**The Diet Delusion**'. This huge, impressive book is a staggering achievement. It is incredibly detailed and goes into fascinating depth about every aspect of diet and nutritional research. It's a lot to get through but it does contain many gems. For example, I learned that the man who came up with the term 'vitamins' was called Casimir Funk, which has to be one of the greatest names in history. It's a shame it's not also a style of music.

Turner, Gary. '**No Worries**'. If you want to overcome anxiety, worry and related negative feelings, I highly recommend this book. Full disclosure: I helped Gary to write this book but all the content is his and I don't make any money from sales.

Wolf, Naomi. '**The Beauty Myth**'. The subtitle says it all: 'How Images Of Beauty Are Used Against Women'. A superb book in every respect and one that every man should read.

Yudkin, John. '**Pure, White And Deadly**'. The 1972 book that raised the alarm regarding the dangers of dietary sucrose. Very controversial in its day, with Yudkin being denounced as either a heretic or an idiot. Time has been kinder to Yudkin's thesis than to all of his (very vocal) critics.

What Can I Do For You?

Personal Coaching And Training

I work with private clients all over the world, either in person or via the internet. Some people ask me for help with weight loss and fitness. Others want a little help with self-fulfilment and personal success, building their business, creating a passive income or related subjects. Let's work together and see what value I can provide for you!

See any of my websites for details.

Talks, Keynotes And Corporate Training

I love taking part in live events! I offer excellent talks, training and keynotes on subjects such as persuasion and communication skills, working for yourself, creating digital products and building a passive income. I often add touches of magic and mindreading, just to make my sessions a little bit different!

To date, I've worked for the FBI, Google, Coca-Cola, Marks & Spencer, The British Olympics Team, The Ministry of Defence, Hewlett-Packard, The Philadelphia 76ers, CapGemini, BBC, Kier Construction, NBC, The Crown Estate, Iceland, Medtronic, Unilever, The Sunday Times Oxford Literary Festival, The Prince's Charities, McKinsey & Company, Eurostar Software Testing Conference, Ogilvy & Mather, Rabobank, London Business School, ABC Television, Channel 4, Cambridge Technology Partners, Synon, Valtech and many other companies.

I've also lectured at Oxford University, Cambridge University, the California Institute of Technology and Monash University.

Writing

A friend once described me as 'a book midwife'. If you have a book in you, I'll help you to write it, publish it yourself, market it and make some money from it. I've been a professional writer for over 35 years and I offer a complete, end-to-end service.

I particularly like helping people to create a passive income for themselves: create a product, set up a website, make money while you sleep. This is what I've been doing for about twenty years. I can guide you through the entire process! It's a challenging road to travel, to be sure, but at the same time highly satisfying and rewarding.

Social Media

I'd love to stay in touch via social media!

For each of my main websites, there is a corresponding Facebook page:

www.ianrowland.com
www.theaddictionfixer.com
www.coldreadingsuccess.com

You can also find me on:
Twitter (@IanRowland1)
Linked In
Instagram

Some Kind Words...

"My FBI Behavioural Analysis Program hired Ian to work with and train our team for a full day. He demonstrated and taught us a lot about cold reading and how we could apply it to our work as behavioural analysts. Additionally, he also covered advanced communication skills, persuasive language and relevant insights into the art of 'misdirection'. At the conclusion of his comprehensive seminar, he entertained our entire team and families with a mindreading show at an evening social. Not only was it great fun, but even today my team is still talking about it. I'd highly recommend Ian to anyone who's interested in these subjects and wants a first-class speaker and trainer."
— *Robin Dreeke, former Special Agent and Head of* **FBI Behavioural Analysis Program**

"I regard Ian as a first-rate trainer and consultant. He has amazing material, he always delivers and he's great to work with."
— *A. Sanghi, Lead Economist,* **World Bank Group**

"Ian has a very engaging and energising style and he was thought-provoking and entertaining throughout. Most importantly, everyone said it was a great use of their time. Ian gave us plenty of ways to work smarter and be more effective both professionally and personally."
— *A. Mellor,* **Marks & Spencer**

"Ian is the best speaker and trainer I've ever seen, and he hosted our day perfectly. We learned a lot, he was entertaining and I know we'll be more successful this year thanks to what he shared with us."
— *D. Holmes, Financial Director,* **Healthcare Learning**

"*We had some of the top experts around the globe in their field, but when we looked at how people were registering for the conference and what the attendees wanted, overwhelmingly we saw very large numbers signing up for Ian's course, so much so that his class was the largest in the whole session that we had for those three days.*"
— *Chris Hadnagy,* **Organiser, Human Hacking Conference**

"Of the hundred plus lectures and shows we have hosted at Caltech none have brought more enthusiastic praise than your performance. I have now heard from dozens of people in the audience, all of whom said this was one of the most entertaining, informative, and above all funny shows they had ever seen. You are to be congratulated for breathing so much life and class into the science and skeptics community."
— *Michael Shermer,* **Executive Director, Skeptics Society**

"Ian's special talent lies in his ability to communicate useful information about self-improvement, business, psychology and, yes, magic to diverse audiences around the world. His books are essential reading and if you get the opportunity to hear him speak, don't miss him! For those outside the world of magic and mindreading, let me tell you that Ian is very highly regarded in the trade. He even gets hired to go to major conventions and teach other magicians! When I was Editor of the Magic Circle's magazine, I asked Ian to write a column on mindreading, which he did for 12 years to great acclaim."
— *Matthew Field,* **Member of the Inner Magic Circle**

"I've been an Independent Financial Advisor for 20 years and have learned from people like Dale Carnegie, Anthony Robbins, Jim Rohn and Brian Tracy. I now include Ian Rowland on that list. Having attended his courses and invested in some personal coaching with him, I cannot recommend him highly enough. His unique insights regarding positive persuasion and what makes people tick will prove invaluable in your personal and business life. He's funny, engaging and a leader in his field."
— *Mike LeGassick,* **Leading Independent Financial Advisor**, *UK*

"I make it my business to learn from experts. I spent four days with Ian and we covered a range of skills that I know will help me both personally and professionally — particularly inter-personal skills and ways to establish instant rapport with people. I think he's terrific."
— *Sam Q.,* **Entrepreneur**, *Saudi Arabia*

"I'm a sales guy. I've studied all the big names and been trained by some of the best in the business. I trained with Ian via Skype and he just blew my mind with techniques and perspectives I never knew before. It's all practical. I use what Ian taught me almost every day. He opened my eyes to aspects of communication that truly deserve the term 'magic'."
— *Michael Martin,* **Sales professional**, *USA*

"I studied CRFB with Ian via Skype and without doubt it's my best investment this year! Ian is an excellent teacher and working with him is very enjoyable. In addition, Ian is incredibly generous with his knowledge in many adjacent fields.
— *Patrick Ehrich,* **Teacher and Educational Trainer**, *Germany*

Printed in Poland
by Amazon Fulfillment
Poland Sp. z o.o., Wrocław

59210470R00085